Weather to Sail

The Complete Guide to Sailing Weather

Weather to Sail

The Complete Guide to Sailing Weather

MIKE BRETTLE
AND BRIDGET SMITH

The Crowood Press

First published in 1999 by
The Crowood Press Ltd
Ramsbury, Marlborough
Wiltshire SN8 2HR

British Library Cataloguing in Publication Data
A catalogue record for this book is available from the British Library.

ISBN 1 86126 295 7

Photograph previous page: satellite photograph of Britain and northwest Europe taken at 0830UTC on 27
September 1987.

Acknowledgements
Thanks are due to Dorry Glockling, Frank Glockling, Bob Leonard, Malcolm MacVean, Mike Molyneux and
Glenn Shutts for very helpful comments on the manuscript. Robert Hope of Greenham Marine and Alan
Davies of Brookes and Gatehouse Ltd gave useful specialist advice on parts of Chapter 9. The National
Meteorology Library provided valuable assistance with various charts and publications. The shipping
forecasts and analysed charts in Chapter 8 are reproduced with permission of the Controller of HMSO and
are Crown Copyright. The frontispiece is reproduced with kind permission of the University of Dundee
and the cloud photographs in Figs 9, 10 and 58 are reproduced by courtesy of Storm Dunlop.

Additional photographs are reproduced by courtesy of Westerly Group Ltd, WNI Oceanroutes Ltd, Newstel
Information Ltd, Roberts Radio Ltd, Prosser Scientific Instruments Ltd and Raytheon Marine Company.

Special thanks are due to Jim Glockling who produced most of the drawings.

The weather chart on the front cover is reproduced with permission of the controller of HMSO. Cover
photographs by Westerly Group Ltd and Brookes and Gatehouse Ltd.

Dedication
To the late M.A. Giblett, Superintendent of the Airship Division of the Meteorological Office.

Font used: Melior.

Typeset and designed by D & N Publishing
Membury Business Park, Lambourn Woodlands
Hungerford, Berkshire.

Printed and bound by JW Arrowsmith, Bristol.

CONTENTS

1
WEATHER SYSTEMS

Surface Pressure

The most obvious feature of a weather map is the pattern of lines, called isobars, which join points of equal atmospheric pressure. The atmospheric pressure at a particular point on Earth is nothing more or less than the weight of atmosphere above it. Pressure will fall with height simply because at higher levels there is less atmosphere above. The pressure indicated on weather charts is sea-level pressure which is convenient for meteorological analysis as it eliminates any possible artificial distortion of weather features caused by the varying altitudes of different reporting stations. Observing stations, manned observatories, automatic weather stations, airports and so on, will correct their pressure readings according to their height above mean sea level. The correction will vary with ambient temperature since cold air is denser than warm air.

Pressure and Wind

To understand wind and why it varies with time and place we must be aware of the forces that act on air in the atmosphere. The most important of these is the

Units of Pressure

The standard unit of pressure used by meteorologists is the hectopascal which is abbreviated to hPa. It is based on the SI (Systeme International) system of units which is the most commonly used worldwide. In the SI system, the Pascal is the unit of pressure (force per square metre) and one hectopascal represents a pressure of one hundred Pascals. Fortunately, the hectopascal is exactly equal to the millibar (mb), which it is gradually replacing. The millibar is based on an older system in which one bar nominally represents mean sea-level pressure, and since one millibar is one thousandth of a bar, mean sea-level pressure is roughly 1000mb. Bars are still widely used as a unit of pressure in some fields. Other units that might be encountered, especially on older barometers or barographs, are inches or millimetres of mercury. Millimetres of mercury are still occasionally used as a pressure unit for aviation. These units go back to the old-style mercury barometers which operated using a column of mercury balanced against the pressure of the atmosphere. It is an interesting thought that a column of mercury only about 760mm in height weighs as much as the same cross-section column the entire depth of the atmosphere. Most almanacs will have a conversion table so that measurements in these older units can be compared and converted to the more modern units used in broadcast forecasts.

pressure gradient. Air pressure varies from place to place and so air will be subject to a horizontal force acting from high to low pressure.

The other main factor influencing wind on a large scale is the Coriolis effect. This results from the Earth's rotation and is rather more complex than the pressure gradient. Air moving across a rotating Earth behaves as though a force were deflecting it, to the right in the northern hemisphere and to the left in the southern hemisphere. The size of the effect varies with latitude, being strongest at the poles and non-existent at the equator. It also varies with wind speed. Contrary to popular belief, the Coriolis effect is not relevant to water going down a plughole in a domestic bath although it does influence tides.

In order to understand the way in which pressure and the Coriolis effect interact to produce the large-scale wind flow over the Earth consider, for example, a mass of air in the northern hemisphere forced to accelerate by the pressure gradient from high to low pressure. As the air accelerates it will experience an increasing Coriolis effect pulling it to the right. Eventually, a balance is reached when the air no longer moves from high to low pressure but in a direction such that lower pressure is to the left of the direction of travel and the horizontal pressure gradient exactly compensates for the Coriolis effect (*see* Fig. 1).

The Size of the Coriolis Effect

According to urban myth, the direction which water takes in going down the plughole of a domestic bath is determined by the Coriolis effect and is different in the northern and southern hemispheres. Unfortunately, this is not the case; the flow of water down plugholes is determined by the shape of the bath and the rotation picked up by the water as the bath was filled. The Coriolis effect does, however, produce a noticeable effect on water occurring in bulk, such as tides. It is also an important consideration for the accurate control of long-range rockets and gunnery, so much so that naval vessels and artillery units have to make allowances for it when operating at different latitudes.

The magnitude of the Coriolis effect can be illustrated by the following consideration. A strong horizontal pressure gradient in the atmosphere might be 5hPa over 100km (62 miles). This gradient would, if balanced by the Coriolis effect in mid latitudes, give a geostrophic wind of about 60kt. However, 5hPa is equivalent to the pressure fall occurring over a height of only about 40m (130ft) in the atmosphere. The Coriolis effect is typically equivalent to a horizontal pressure gradient over 2,000 times smaller than the vertical pressure gradient. This small effect can nevertheless determine the pattern of atmospheric circulation on the grand scale.

Books on meteorology usually state that the Coriolis effect is absent at the equator, but this is not strictly true. The effect operates at right angles to the axis of rotation of the Earth. Therefore, the full effect is horizontal at the poles and it is here that it has the most effect on horizontal movement. At the equator the Coriolis effect works vertically and has no effect on horizontal motion. It is still present, however, and in some extremely sensitive applications meteorologists may have to allow for it even though it is overwhelmed by the vertical pressure gradient. If the entire atmosphere moves eastwards at 20kt near to the equator then the Coriolis effect would reduce the surface pressure by about 0.1hPa. Similarly, westward motion would increase it by the same amount. For most practical purposes it is negligible and is less than the pressure fall over 1m of height near to the Earth's surface.

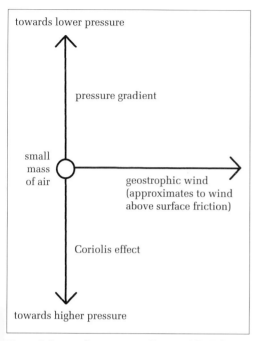

towards lower pressure

pressure gradient

small
mass
of air

geostrophic wind
(approximates to wind
above surface friction)

Coriolis effect

towards higher pressure

Fig. 1 Balance of pressure gradient and Coriolis effect in the northern hemisphere.

This example, though simple, does help to explain how wind is related to the pressure patterns in the atmosphere. Figure 2 illustrates approximate wind flow around various large-scale weather features. (At the equator the Coriolis effect is generally accepted as being non-existent and wind patterns are based on a very different set of rules.) The steeper the pressure gradient, that is, the more rapidly the pressure changes with distance, the faster the air has to move to be balanced by the Coriolis effect. Thus, a steep pressure gradient gives stronger winds than a shallow pressure gradient. The wind resulting from the combination of Coriolis effect and pressure gradient is called the geostrophic wind (meaning 'earth turning').

By analogy with contour lines on a conventional land map, features on weather maps are named after geographical features, such as cols and ridges. Figure 2 shows some of these features and their associated isobar patterns. The isobar spacing represents the pressure gradient so that closely spaced isobars are indicative of a steeper pressure gradient just as closely spaced contour lines on a land map indicate a steep slope. Since a steeper pressure gradient results in a higher geostrophic wind speed it follows that isobar spacing gives useful clues to windspeed. In Fig. 2, the wind will be stronger at point A than at point B. It can also be clearly seen how lower surface pressure is always to the left of the direction of the wind (in the northern hemisphere). This is the basis of Buys Ballot's Law which gives a simple link between everyday experience and large-scale weather systems. It states that, when standing on reasonably exposed ground or sailing on open water and facing downwind, lower pressure will be in a direction to the left in the northern hemisphere. Sometimes weather charts showing isobars include a small scale called the geostrophic wind scale. This allows for a quick assessment of the wind that would result from just the pressure gradient and the Coriolis effect. The wind speed is calculated by measuring the separation between isobars at a point of interest and then transferring this value to the scale at the appropriate latitude. In Fig. 2, the geostrophic wind speed at point A (latitude 50°N) is 40kt.

Strictly speaking, the geostrophic wind value is only valid for situations of steady, uniform flow in a straight line clear of the influence of surface friction. The geostrophic wind scales on charts are also produced for a standard atmosphere with a surface pressure of about 1,013 hectopascals (hPa) and a temperature of 15°

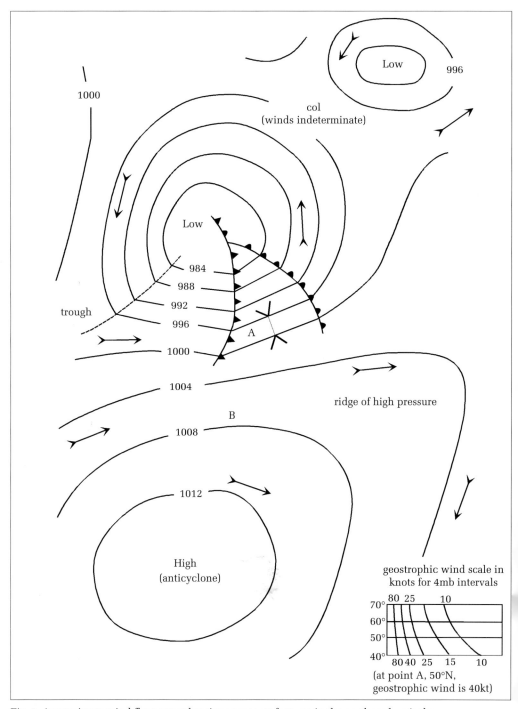

Fig. 2 Approximate wind flow around various pressure features in the northern hemisphere.

Celsius. Typical variations in surface pressure and temperature can affect the geostrophic wind by about 10 per cent. Despite these limitations, the geostrophic wind is a useful concept and is widely used to estimate roughly the wind speed and direction near to the surface but clear of surface friction. The wind at 900m determined from a weather balloon is often taken by meteorologists as being the geostrophic wind. Obviously the actual surface wind will be different for several reasons, the most important of these being friction at the surface.

Surface Friction

At the Earth's surface, the wind is significantly altered by the effects of surface friction. As might be expected, speed is reduced but the direction is also altered. This change in direction is a consequence of the reduction in speed. The pressure gradient is the same whatever the wind speed, but the Coriolis effect is reduced if wind speed is reduced. The addition of a frictional force or drag usually causes the surface wind to be backed anticlockwise relative to that aloft (*see* Fig. 3). In the southern hemisphere the surface wind is veered clockwise to that aloft. (In meteorology, 'veer' means a clockwise change in direction and 'back' means an anticlockwise change in direction.) The size of the change in direction varies according to a number of factors. It is greater the further one is from the equator and also over rougher surfaces. The temperature structure of the lower atmosphere is also a major factor; indeed, the variation in temperature with height near the Earth's surface can contribute significantly to sailing conditions. The surface wind over the sea

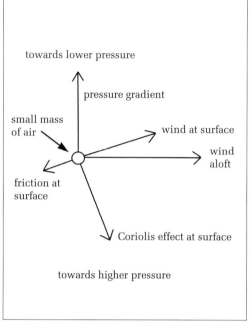

Fig. 3 Balance of pressure gradient, Coriolis effect and surface friction near the surface in the northern hemisphere.

is about 70 to 80 per cent of the geostrophic value and is backed by about 10 degrees. These values are included here with some reluctance, however, as variations from one case to another can be significant. Over land, useful estimates of the effect of friction are even more difficult to define as they depend on the terrain.

Ascent and Descent in Highs and Lows

Surface friction not only reduces wind speed at the surface but also changes the wind direction, which has dramatic consequences for the associated weather. Wind around a region of low pressure in

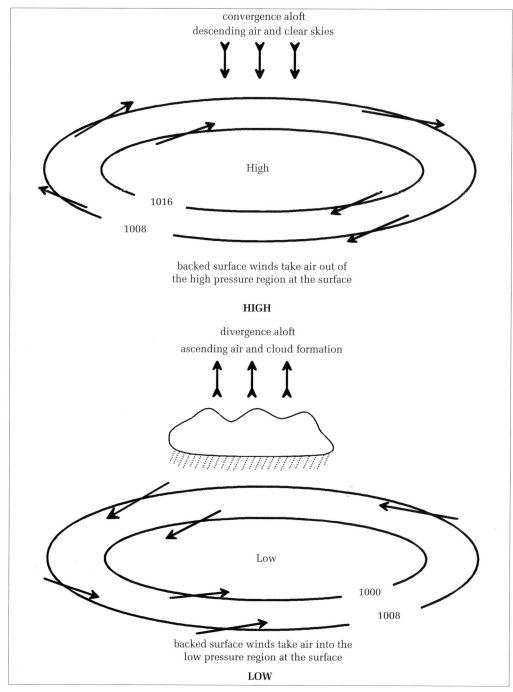

Fig. 4 Descending and ascending air associated with stable high- and low-pressure regions in the northern hemisphere.

the northern hemisphere will be backed at the surface relative to that aloft and will be veered in the southern hemisphere. This means that there is a tendency for the surface wind to spiral in towards lower pressure. If the low pressure is persisting or deepening, it follows that air entering the low at the surface must be ascending within the region and leaving at a higher level. In meteorological terms, the air is said to be converging at the surface and diverging at higher levels. Figure 4 shows the resulting pattern associated with a low-pressure and a high-pressure region. The pattern around the high-pressure region, sometimes called an anticyclone, is essentially the reverse of the low. In the southern hemisphere air also descends in highs and ascends in lows since the wind direction for a given pressure pattern is reversed, despite the wind being veered at the surface. The level at which there is neither convergence nor divergence is usually called the level of no divergence and is typically found at about 5km (3 miles) altitude.

As air rises in a low-pressure region it cools, which results in the formation of cloud and subsequent precipitation. In a high-pressure region, descending air warms and so cloud evaporates. Thus low pressure is commonly associated with bad weather and high pressure with fair weather. An isolated region of low or high pressure is not essential for this process to occur. Common examples of the effects described include the troughs of low pressure which result in some of the worst weather around depressions, and ridges of high pressure such as those which often extend from the Azores to Western Europe, giving fair conditions during the summer. Of course, high pressure does not always mean good weather. A side effect of the descending air within a high pressure region is a blocking of any movement of polluted air, leading to a deterioration in air quality. In winter, descending air can be cooled on approaching the ground so that the calm, foggy, overcast and damp conditions known as an anticyclonic gloom develop.

Atmospheric Stability

It is commonly accepted that warm air rises and also that temperature falls with height. This obviously begs the question, 'Why doesn't the warm air at the surface ascend, and replace the cooler air above?' The explanation for this paradox is based on the fall in pressure that accompanies the rise of warm air from the surface. Imagine a small volume of air rising, perhaps as a result of minor turbulence (see Fig. 5). As the air rises, its pressure falls simply because there is now less weight of atmosphere above. This fall in pressure causes the air to expand and cool due to the inter-relationship of pressure, temperature and volume for a fixed amount of a gas. The rate at which air cools if it is forced upwards is known as the dry adiabatic lapse rate (DALR), and near to the surface this is about ten degrees Celsius per kilometre. If the temperature fall with height in the real atmosphere is the same as the DALR, then the atmosphere is said to have neutral stability. This means that any air which is lifted or lowered by whatever means will remain at the same temperature as the surrounding air. It would, therefore, have no tendency to carry on rising or falling or to return to its original position. The actual rate of change with height is called the environmental lapse rate. If the environmental lapse rate is less than the DALR, then air displaced upwards will be cooler and denser than its surroundings, and so will sink back down to its former level (*see* Fig. 6). Similarly, air displaced downwards will be warmed, because of the increasing pressure, to a higher temperature than the surroundings and will therefore tend to rise back to its former level. In this case, the atmosphere is said to be stable because it resists vertical motion. Note that it is not necessary for temperature actually to increase with height, as in an inversion, for the air to be stable.

The opposite of a stable atmosphere is an unstable atmosphere (*see* Fig. 6). In this situation the variation in temperature with height is such that, if air is displaced upwards, the fall in temperature will still leave it warmer than its surroundings. It will therefore be less dense than the surroundings and the upward motion will continue. Similarly, air displaced downwards will be warmed as a result of the increasing pressure, but will still be cooler than the surroundings and will continue to sink. In this case, the atmosphere is said to be unstable because it encourages vertical motion.

Stability and Wind

The practical significance of the stability of the atmosphere results from its effect on the amount of air movement between levels that takes place near the surface. If the air is unstable, there will be relatively

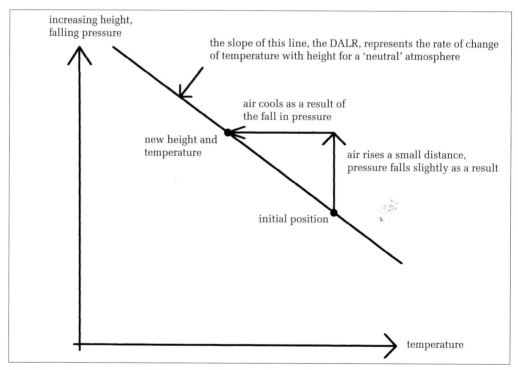

increasing height, falling pressure

the slope of this line, the DALR, represents the rate of change of temperature with height for a 'neutral' atmosphere

air cools as a result of the fall in pressure

new height and temperature

air rises a small distance, pressure falls slightly as a result

initial position

temperature

Fig. 5 How the temperature of air changes if it is forced upwards.

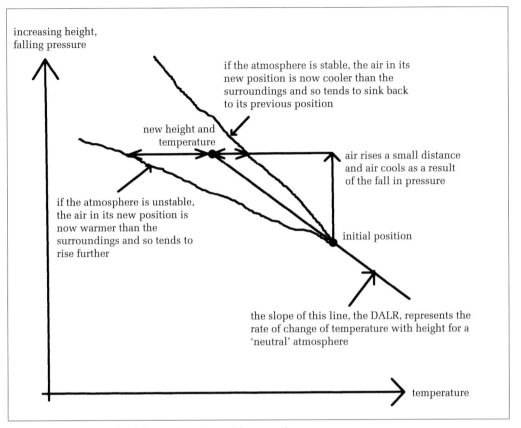

increasing height,
falling pressure

if the atmosphere is stable, the air in its
new position is now cooler than the
surroundings and so tends to sink back
to its previous position

new height and
temperature

air rises a small distance
and air cools as a result
of the fall in pressure

if the atmosphere is unstable,
the air in its new position is
now warmer than the
surroundings and so tends to
rise further

initial position

the slope of this line, the DALR, represents the
rate of change of temperature with height for a
'neutral' atmosphere

temperature

Fig. 6 Temperature profiles for stable and unstable atmospheres.

more movement and more frequent and larger gusts. The mean wind near the surface will be stronger for the same geostrophic wind. This results from the increased mixing which will tend to reduce the variation in mean wind speed with height. Another effect of increased mixing is that the mean wind direction will not change much with height. Figure 3 has shown how the direction changes at the surface due to friction. If the air is unstable, the mean wind near the surface will be closer to the geostrophic wind in direction as well as speed (although variations in gusts may be very much larger).

Table 1 (*see* overleaf) shows a comparison between winds at the surface (nominal 10m), and at 900m, over London Heathrow Airport, UK, and over Ocean Weather Ships I and J, for stable and unstable atmospheres. (When this data was collected Heathrow and OWS I and J both operated a programme of weather balloon ascents so the change in temperature with height was measured directly.) From the table we can see that surface winds tend to be backed further from geostrophic wind as a result of the greater friction over land than sea for equivalent stability. Although it may not be obvious,

Table 1

Summary of angle (degrees) between surface
and geostrophic winds (taken as the wind at
900m, for London Heathrow Airport, UK, and
Ocean Weather Ships (OWS) I and J (at 59°N
19°W and 52°N 20°W)) for stable and
unstable conditions

	Heathrow	OWS I and J
Unstable	5°	0°
Stable	30°–35°	15°–20°

many studies have shown that in terms of
the drag imposed on the wind, the sea is
invariably less rough than the land. Surprisingly, the waves caused by a force six
wind in the Solent are, to the atmosphere,
smoother than a cricket pitch. It can also
be seen from Table 1 that in unstable conditions the mean surface wind is much
more closely aligned with the geostrophic
wind irrespective of surface roughness.

Fronts and Frontal Depressions

Apart from isobars, weather fronts are the
most obvious feature of weather maps.
The easiest way to explain the nature of
fronts is by following the formation and
life cycle of a frontal depression. These
features often seem to dominate the
weather of temperate latitudes, because
these latitudes mark the approximate
boundary between cold polar air and
warmer air to the south. The boundary is
called the polar front, but since it is unstable it rarely exists as a distinct structure.
It usually consists of a line of vortices several hundred miles across known as
frontal depressions. Pressure is lower in

the centre of these features consistent
with the direction of airflow around them
near to the surface. Asking whether the
low pressure causes the airflow or vice
versa is a bit of a chicken-and-egg question, and in practice the pressure and
wind fields develop together.

The manner in which frontal depressions are formed is illustrated in Fig. 7.
Initially, a wave forms on the polar front
and cold air moves south. The boundary
between the cold air moving south and the
warm air is a cold front. Warm air moving
north forms a warm front. Warm fronts are
marked on charts with semicircles and
cold fronts with triangles. These point in
the direction of the movement of the front.
Although fronts are shown on charts as a
single line, the surface between the cold
and warm air slopes at a very shallow
angle, typically one in two hundred for a
warm front, and one in fifty for a cold front.
The line shown on a chart marks the position of the front at the surface. Figure 8
shows cross-sections through warm and
cold fronts. The cloud structure is somewhat idealized and fronts rarely follow the
exact textbook form. Nevertheless, some
knowledge of cloud types can be useful as
well as interesting, and will give an idea of
where the observer stands in relation to the
overall weather pattern. In particular, the
veil of high cirrus or cirrostratus cloud that
is often seen ahead of an advancing warm
front has long been regarded as a sign of
bad weather. The shallow slope of a warm
front means that the clouds are observed
well ahead of the surface feature.

The appearance of the main types of
cloud associated with weather fronts are
shown in Figs 9 to 14, and their location
within warm and cold fronts is illustrated
in Fig. 8. This figure also demonstrates the
distinct ways in which clouds are created

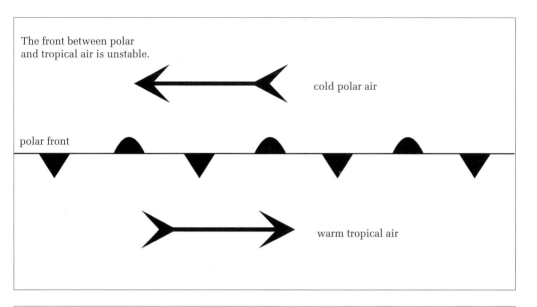

The front between polar
and tropical air is unstable.

cold polar air

polar front

warm tropical air

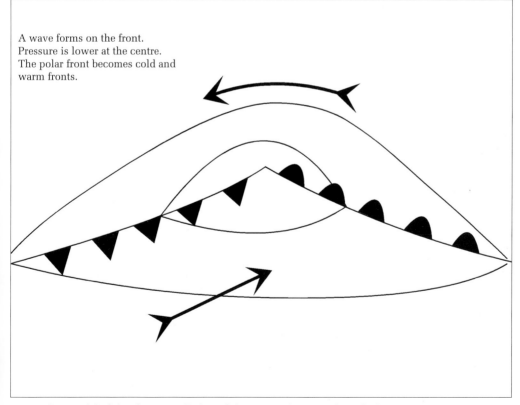

A wave forms on the front.
Pressure is lower at the centre.
The polar front becomes cold and
warm fronts.

Fig. 7 The simplified development of a frontal depression (continued overleaf).

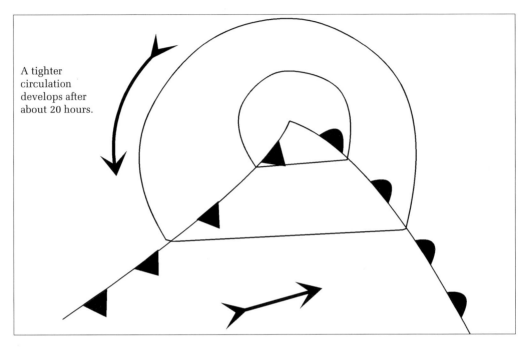

A tighter circulation develops after about 20 hours.

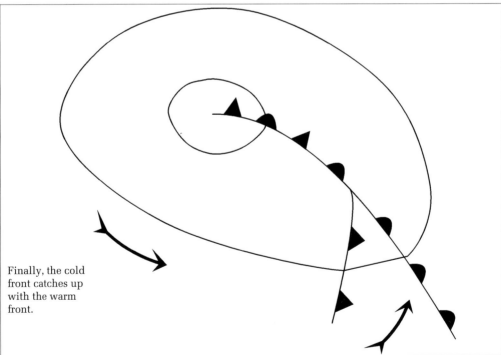

Finally, the cold front catches up with the warm front.

Fig. 7 The simplified development of a frontal depression (continued).

within warm and cold fronts. The warm-front clouds result from warm, moist air rising up over the colder air ahead and subsequently cooling. This causes condensation which in turn creates layer clouds and precipitation over a large area. Warm-front precipitation is therefore usually continuous, but not necessarily heavy. The precipitation may sometimes vary in intensity with the passage of heavier bands. Cold fronts are associated with more vigorous, showery precipitation from deeper clouds. This results from the instability of the air behind the cold front, since its source is cold and it will have been travelling over relatively warm surfaces for some time. This means that it has been warmed from below, giving a more rapid fall in temperature with height. Figure 15 shows the distribution of clouds around simplified warm and cold fronts. It can clearly be seen how the first signs of

the warm front occur hundreds of miles ahead of it and even the first precipitation is over 100 miles (160km) in front. The cold front, on the other hand, arrives unannounced since it arrives at the surface first, sliding under the warmer air ahead. The observer on the ground gets little or no warning of the cold front until, on passing, the wind veers, probably in a sequence of gusts, and typically the sky clears within a period of tens of minutes. An important feature to emphasize is the change in wind direction when a front passes. This is shown by the patterns of isobars and the kink in the isobars at the fronts. In the northern hemisphere the wind direction veers (changes clockwise), and in the southern hemisphere it backs (changes anticlockwise). Changes in the wind at the cold front are likely to be the most dramatic and may occur in a sequence of gusts or squalls. The geostrophic wind can be a

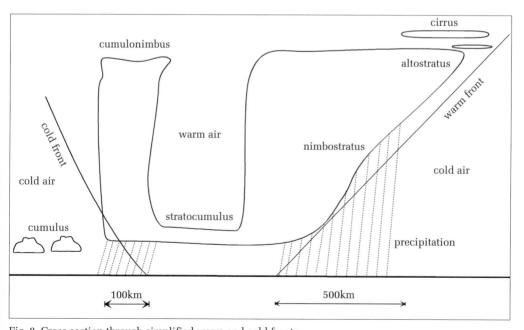

Fig. 8 Cross-section through simplified warm and cold fronts.

Fig. 9 Cumulus clouds. These are the characteristic clouds of the cold sector of a frontal depression. They are also found in high pressure regions. Small cumulus clouds, such as these, are sometimes referred to as fair weather cumulus although larger cumulus can cause showers. The cumulus clouds in this picture are arranged in lines, or 'streets'.

useful concept for the amateur forecaster studying fronts as it gives a rough approximation of the speed at which the front is moving. Some weather charts give special scales which may allow for a more accurate approximation of the front speed than the straightforward geostrophic wind (Fig. 16). They can, for instance, allow for the fact that cold fronts generally move faster than the associated warm front.

Professional meteorologists subdivide fronts, referring to active fronts, ana-fronts, kata-fronts, and so on. There are also some distinguished meteorologists who, after a great deal of research, have concluded that the simple model of fronts that is presented in popular weather guides (such as this one!), may be so over-simplified as to do more harm than good. Modern meteorological jargon refers to

warm and cold conveyor belts moving air between different levels of the atmosphere, as well as over the surface of the Earth. Having said this, forecasts and charts available to yachtsmen refer to the traditional models and so they should be aware of what to expect from them.

Apart from warm and cold fronts, occluded fronts are also important. They take various forms, but generally result from a cold front catching up with a warm front to leave an elevated region of cloud along a trough of low pressure. As with other fronts or troughs, the wind is likely to veer in the northern hemisphere as an occluded front passes. There are two main forms of occluded front, namely cold occlusions and warm occlusions. The yachtsman should be aware of this distinction as they behave in quite different

Fig. 10 Cumulonimbus clouds. These are an extreme development of cumulus clouds. They form when cumulus clouds develop to such a height that the top falls below about –10°C. At this point, the water drops start to freeze and the characteristic anvil top forms. Found in unstable air, such as in cold northerly airstreams or at vigorous cold fronts, they produce showers, gusts or squalls, and possibly thunderstorms.

Fig. 11 Cirrus clouds, and the similar cirrostratus and cirrocumulus, are high level ice clouds. They may be associated with approaching frontal depressions, appearing hundreds of miles ahead of a warm front or warm occlusion, or may be of little significance. They sometimes produce various optical phenomena, such as haloes (rings around the sun or moon).

Fig. 12 Altostratus cloud. This is a medium level cloud characteristic of approaching frontal systems. It may be so thin that the sun is visible giving a 'ground glass' effect. A classic sign of approaching bad weather is the progressive descent and thickening of the cloud base. This develops from a high veil of cirrus or cirrostratus to thickening altostratus, which eventually obscures the sun.

Fig. 13 Nimbostratus cloud. Nimbostratus is a layer cloud producing precipitation in the form of rain, sleet or snow. It is most commonly associated with the arrival of a warm front or occlusion. At the time of this picture, there was a steady fall of light rain.

ways. Figure 17 shows cross-sections through cold and warm occlusions. If the cold air behind the front is cooler than the air ahead of it, the front behaves somewhat similarly to a cold front, and if it is less cool then the occlusion behaves similarly to a warm front. There is another important difference to be noted in that surface charts show the line of an occlusion as the intersection of the front with the surface. If the occlusion is a cold occlusion then the region of elevated warm air will be behind the surface front, thus giving the cold occlusion the element of surprise associated with cold fronts. A warm occlusion is a more drawn-out affair that is similar to a warm front. The two types can be distinguished on a chart because a cold occlusion appears as an extension of the cold front and a warm occlusion as an extension of the warm front in the system. Generally speaking, cold occlusions predominate over the British Isles. Figure 17 also shows the different structures of cold and warm occlusions. The elevated wedge of warm air associated with an occlusion is sometimes marked on charts and may be labelled as a TROWAL (TROugh of Warm air ALoft).

Fronts are important features of mid-latitude weather and rightly get a lot of attention in textbooks and forecasts. However, yachtsmen should be aware that they are only a basic model of a complex phenomenon.

Fig. 14 Stratocumulus cloud. This is a low level cloud. It is probably the most common cloud in the UK and is associated with the warm sector of a depression. It may produce precipitation, usually in the form of light continuous rain, drizzle, sleet or snow. These clouds may also be found in winter anticyclones, adding to the effect of 'anticyclonic gloom'.

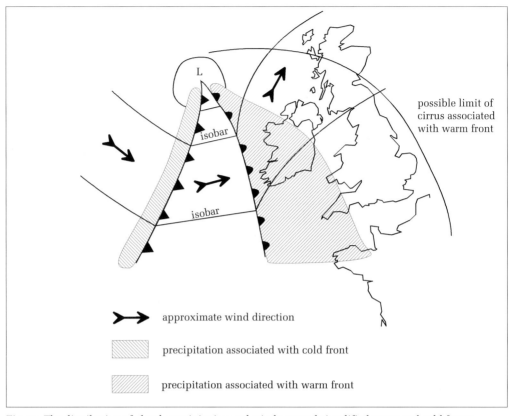

Fig. 15 The distribution of cloud, precipitation and winds around simplified warm and cold fronts.

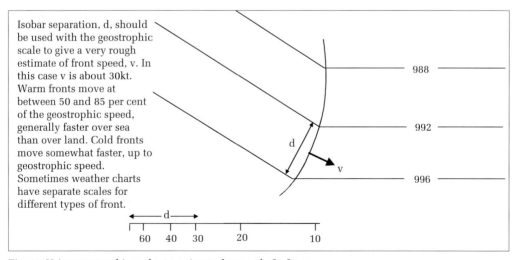

Fig. 16 Using geostrophic scales to estimate the speed of a front.

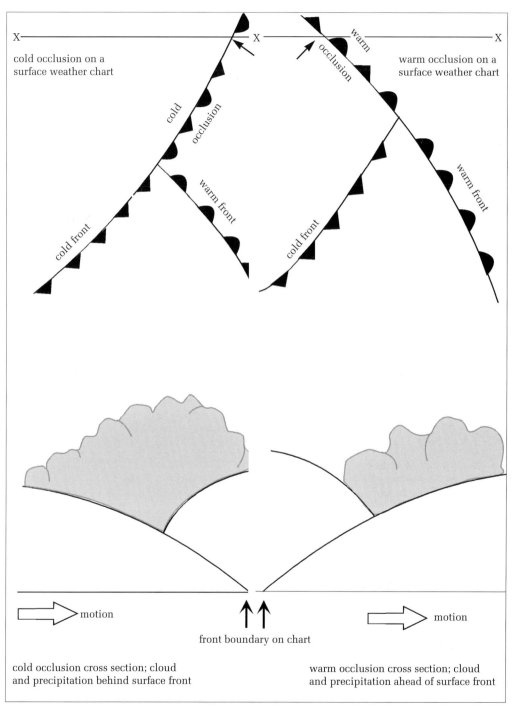

Fig. 17 Cold and warm occluded fronts (occlusions).

Conveyor Belts and Low Level Jets

The current practice of combining radar and satellite imagery has allowed meteorologists a much more detailed view of the structure of certain weather features such as frontal depressions. In recent decades, this has led to a variety of new concepts and hence to increasing scepticism amongst the professionals regarding the simplified descriptions used in the past. This book is not the best place for a full discussion of these issues, except perhaps to make the reader aware that frontal systems are not as clearly understood as one might think and to point out some less well described features which could have a major effect on the weather experienced at sea. The most significant feature of this new analysis is the concept of a 'conveyor belt' of air moving between different layers of the atmosphere. The illustration (*see* Fig. 18) shows a warm conveyor belt of air which starts ahead of a surface cold front at a height of about 1km or less. These conveyor belts

occur in two main forms according to whether the ascent is forward sloping or rearward sloping (note that in this kind of analysis motion is usually referred to relative to the system or front). Figure 18 shows a forward sloping ascent illustrating clearly the differences between the conventional theory and the current analysis.

The main effects on weather for the yachtsman are the low-level 'jets' which run parallel to the cold front. These can exceed 50kt and although they are strongest about 1km above the Earth's surface, they may result in a band of strong surface winds tens of miles wide ahead of the surface cold front. In the case of a forward-sloping ascent, a so-called 'split front' is generated which creates instability and precipitation well ahead of the surface front. The full three-dimensional structure of depressions involves other airflows at higher altitudes, but these are of less relevance to the yachtsman.

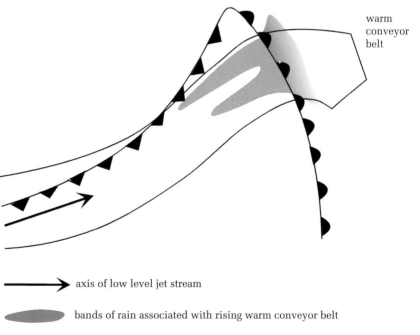

warm conveyor belt

→ axis of low level jet stream

bands of rain associated with rising warm conveyor belt

Fig. 18 A simplified conveyor belt ahead of a surface cold front.

Air Masses

Warm and cold fronts represent boundaries between different types of air mass. A warm front is a boundary between advancing warm air and the cooler air ahead, while a cold front is the reverse of this. Meteorologists, however, define many more types of atmosphere than simply warm or cold. Figure 19 shows the origin of the main air masses that affect the British Isles and Table 2 lists their characteristics.

Upper Winds and the Crosswinds Rule

Wind direction and speed are rarely constant throughout most of the depth of the atmosphere. Figure 20 shows the winds at an altitude of about 30,000ft (9,000m) above a typical frontal depression. The main features are the band of extreme winds in the jet stream and the twist in direction found with height. Ahead of the warm sector of the depression the wind is veering with height and above the cold

Table 2

Characteristics of air masses affecting the British Isles

Type of Air Mass	Characteristics
Arctic Maritime (Am)	Cold, possibly severe in winter. Air passes over a warmer sea surface resulting in showery conditions with exceptional visibility between.
Polar Maritime (Pm)	Cold or cool. Underlying surface is relatively warm. Showery conditions with good visibility between. Typically occurs after passage of cold fronts.
Returning Polar Maritime (rPm)	Normal temperatures. No well-defined cloud type.
Polar Continental (Pc)	Cold in winter, warm in summer except on the east coast. Showery conditions in winter. Generally fair in summer but may result in sea fogs off eastern coasts in spring.
Tropical Continental (Tc)	Very warm, infrequent (accounts for less than 5 per cent of occasions in Britain).
Tropical Maritime (Tm)	Mild with poor visibility. The air is being cooled by the sea below. Dull conditions with precipitation in the form of drizzle or continuous rain. Typically found behind warm fronts.

sector it is backing with height. Such changes are taking place over depths of thousands of feet above the surface and should not be confused with changes in direction near the surface resulting from surface friction. These changes are exam- ples of the general rule that, in the northern hemisphere, winds veering with height are associated with warm advection (advection is the meteorological term for the move- ment of air with a particular characteristic into an area). Likewise, winds backing with

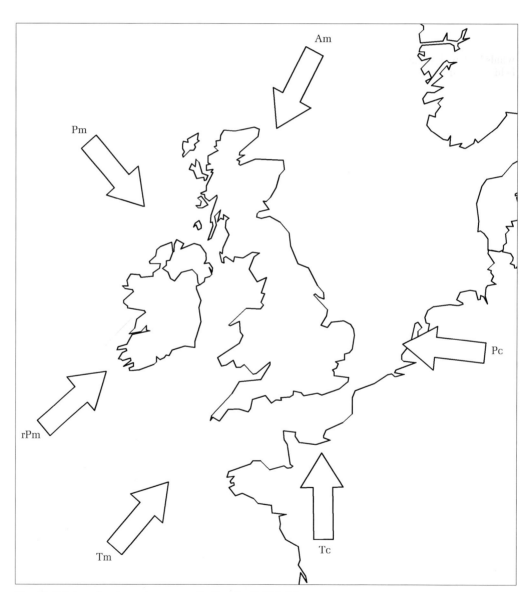

Fig. 19 Origins of various air masses affecting the British Isles.

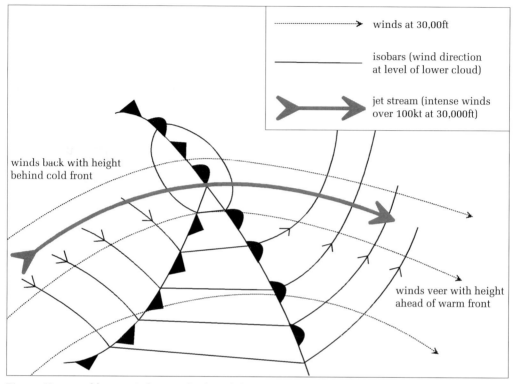

winds at 30,00ft

isobars (wind direction
at level of lower cloud)

jet stream (intense winds
over 100kt at 30,000ft)

winds back with height
behind cold front

winds veer with height
ahead of warm front

Fig. 20 Upper and lower winds around a frontal depression in the northern hemisphere.

height are associated with cold advection. The opposite is the case in the southern hemisphere. The upper winds shown in the diagram are at the height of cirrus clouds. This means that if cirrus clouds are present then these winds can be observed from the surface without special equipment. This is particularly true of cirrus clouds in the jet stream when their motion is often obvious. The wind direction closer to the surface is easily observed if there is some scattered low cloud.

The observations above form the basis for using the crosswinds rule. This states that if the higher clouds show a wind direction veered to that at the surface, then warmer air is advancing, and if they show a direction backed to that at the sur-face, then cold air is advancing. This is correct in the northern hemisphere; in the southern hemisphere the rule is reversed, with winds backing with height implying advancing warm air and winds veering with height implying advancing cold air. The main application is in deter-mining if cirrus clouds observed on a fine day are really due to an approaching warm front and a frontal depression. The rule is less reliable as a warning of cold fronts since a cold front will have already passed by the time the crosswinds are observed. The crosswinds rule may not be used as an alternative to the conven-tional forecasting services, but it is a use-ful exercise for any yachtsman with an interest in meteorology.

Global Wind Patterns

So far, we have only considered wind and weather patterns on the scale of individual depressions and anticyclones, and the air masses affecting the British Isles. These are just part of a global pattern resulting from the imbalance of solar heating between the equator and the poles. Figure 21 shows exactly why the equator is warmer than higher latitudes. This excess heating at the equator has to be balanced by a flow of heat towards the poles which takes place by means of currents in the atmosphere and in the oceans. The currents in the oceans are outside the scope of this book, even though they play a very significant role in weather patterns. In relation to the atmosphere it might be expected that a relatively simple circulation of air would result (*see* Fig. 22). In practice, however, the rotation of the Earth complicates this simple picture. The Coriolis effect appears to prevent the air ever completing its journey towards the poles and so a far more complex pattern results (*see* Fig. 23). An interesting feature of this process is that in the tropics a large proportion of the atmospheric heat is carried in the form of water vapour which, when it condenses to cloud higher up or further from the equator, releases latent heat. The global circulation pattern moves north and south with the seasons and is further distorted by the pattern of continents and

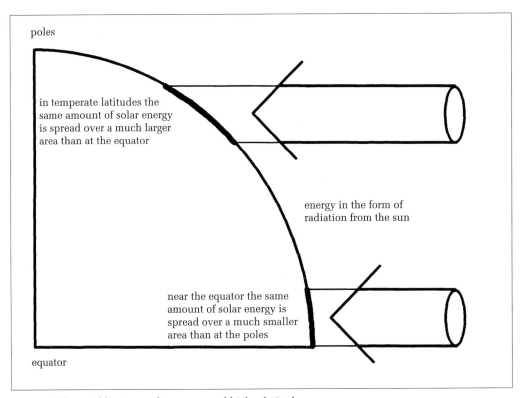

poles

in temperate latitudes the same amount of solar energy is spread over a much larger area than at the equator

energy in the form of radiation from the sun

near the equator the same amount of solar energy is spread over a much smaller area than at the poles

equator

Fig. 21 Differential heating at the equator and higher latitudes.

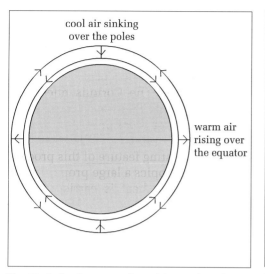

Fig. 22 A simple pattern that might result in the absence of the effects of the Earth's rotation from differential heating at the equator and higher latitudes.

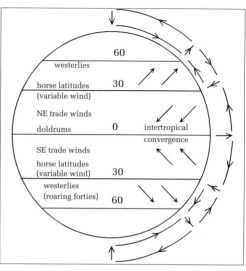

Fig. 23 The basic pattern that results from the effects of the Earth's rotation from differential heating at the equator and higher latitudes.

oceans. Figure 24 shows the final global patterns of surface winds. These are prevailing winds for winter and summer based on the data of many years. At any particular time, the immediate pattern could be quite different.

The doldrums, which are bands of calm winds near to the equator, mark what meteorologists call the 'intertropical convergence zone'. In simple terms, the air in this region is being heated and consequently rises. While the winds at this point are calm, the rising air draws in surface air which, upon being deflected by the Coriolis effect, creates, at around 10 to 20 degrees south, the north-east trade winds. Air at higher levels moving away from the equator completes the circulations. These are called the Hadley Circulations, or Hadley Cells, after the eighteenth-century scientist who first suggested their existence. Further from the equator, between about 30 to 60 degrees

north and south, prevailing westerly winds circle the globe. These are part of the Rossby Circulations (again named after a distinguished scientist). These circulations have some features in common with the adjoining Hadley Cells, but their structure is much less well defined as a result of the presence of frontal depressions which are constantly disturbing the pattern. There are regions of predominantly light and variable wind between these two types of circulation which are known as the Horse Latitudes, apparently because the crews of sailing ships trapped for long periods in these areas would often be forced to slaughter any horse on board for food. In the southern hemisphere the westerly winds run unchecked by any land except for the tip of South America and are known, for obvious reasons, as the Roaring Forties.

The above description of global winds is extremely simplified. In particular, the

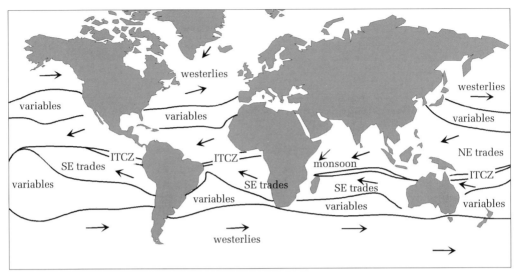

Fig. 24a Actual global wind patterns – January.

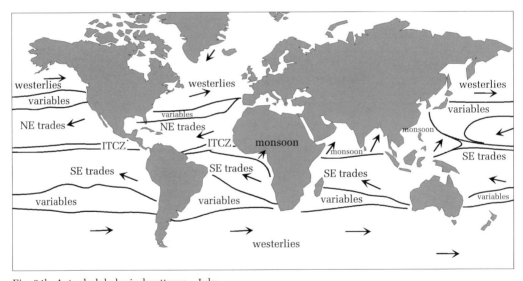

Fig. 24b Actual global wind patterns – July.

regions of light and variable winds are not well defined. Monsoon circulations also dominate over large regions of southern Asia. These are caused by the effects of the huge Asian continent cooling in the northern winter and warming up in the northern summer. The high pressure which results over the Asian continent in winter and the corresponding low pressure in summer generates the prevailing winds and dominates the climate of southern Asia.

2
LOCAL WINDS

Sea and Land Breezes

The sea breeze, familiar to most yachtsmen and inhabitants of coastal regions, is
the cool wind that blows from the sea onto
the land on bright summer afternoons. It
often follows a calm period and may
produce a complete reversal of a light offshore wind. Yachtsmen seeking to understand the sea breeze should begin by
thinking of it as a kind of convection current whereby warm air rises over the land
and cool air sinks over the sea. Since this
mechanism requires the sea to be cooler
than the land, sea breezes generally occur
in the late morning and early afternoon,
and most frequently in early summer
when the sea is at its coolest relative to the
land. Sea temperature does not vary by
much more than a few degrees, changing
slowly over periods of weeks or months,
whereas land temperatures alter by much
larger margins and in far shorter periods
of time. Figure 25 illustrates the basic
mechanism of a sea breeze.

Many guides to forecasting sea breezes
have been published, both for the professional and the layman. Coastal weather stations often have their own varied local
practices, and yachtsmen have been offered
a variety of recommendations on how to
make their own forecasts. Unfortunately,
not enough is known of these circulations
to allow a yachtsman to do more than use
simple rules of thumb to decide whether
a sea breeze will occur on any particular
day. Meteorologists studying sea breezes
are often more concerned with the seaward flow aloft and the inland progres-
sion of the sea-breeze front than the
surface flow offshore. The sea-breeze
front often develops offshore and moves
inshore and then inland.

The tracking of sea-breeze fronts saw
one of the earliest applications of radar to
meteorology. The front itself does not
show up on radar, but sometimes swarms
of swifts, feeding on the insects which
have been taken aloft in the front, produce
strong echoes.

Just as important as the sea-breeze front
to the yachtsman is the anti-front. This
takes the form of a region of calm air at
the surface. Since the air is descending it
is not marked by cloud, but it may produce a noticeable thinning or clearance of
low cloud. Figure 26 shows the basic
wind fields associated with a sea breeze
structure. Although the sea-breeze front
has been studied and observed in great
depth, the anti-front, which is present
with every sea breeze, has merited very

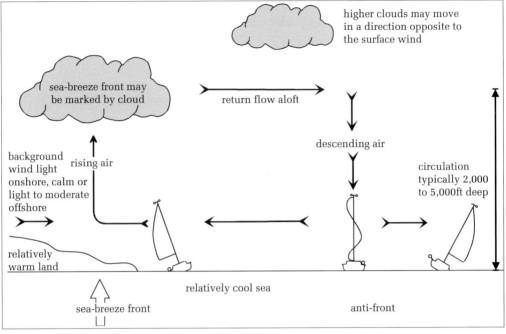

Fig. 25 The basic structure of a developed sea breeze.

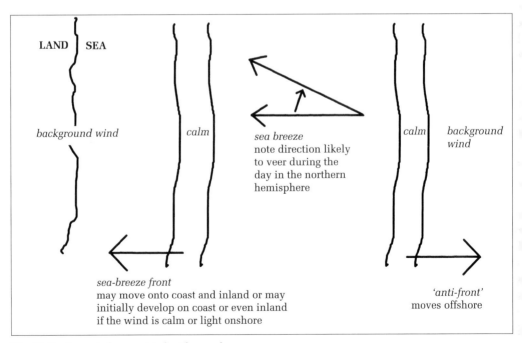

Fig. 26 Surface winds associated with a sea breeze.

little investigation. To a yacht under sail, the anti-front may appear as a barrier of calm air with a complete reversal of wind direction across it. It is definitely something to be aware of when approaching a coastline upwind on a fine day.

Anticipating Sea Breezes

Sea breezes rarely feature in large-scale forecasts for seafarers. A yachtsman has no choice but to decide for him- or herself if sea breezes are going to affect the sailing area. If they do, then they are likely to dominate the situation completely. Relevant sources of information include the shipping forecast which, even if it does not mention sea breezes, will give forecast winds based on the large-scale situation. Since sea breezes require offshore winds, light onshore winds or calm conditions, this is clearly a useful clue. A land forecast mentioning warm inland temperatures or, better still, scattered showers, is indicative of rising air over land and this will generally encourage a sea breeze. The main driving force for the strongest sea breezes is the rapid rise in land surface temperatures under bright sunshine and the resulting convection. Some local radio stations give forecasts and reports which include information on sea temperatures. With all this information to hand, a reliable forecast of sea breezes is quite possible. Thus, with a light offshore wind, a warm afternoon anticipated inland and a cool sea, the yachtsman can expect at around midday to be sailing along the coast in a wind almost opposite to that forecast by the professionals.

In the northern hemisphere the sea breeze is often said to veer clockwise during the day in response to the Coriolis effect. Although this has been confirmed in studies at many locations, it is not universally valid. There is evidence that complicated terrain can influence the sea-breeze structure to such an extent that it will change in the opposite direction and therefore will back during the day. This is something that only local knowledge can resolve, although the odds are that most changes in direction will be in the appropriate direction. In the southern hemisphere the appropriate direction will be backing, and in the tropics there should be no consistent daily change in direction.

In principle, land breezes are the opposite phenomenon to sea breezes. If there is a temperature contrast between land and sea with the sea being warmer, then a circulation will develop with the surface wind flowing offshore and an onshore return flow aloft. In practice, the land breeze is rarely as well defined as the sea breeze. The sun has only to heat a very shallow layer of land to give a large rise in surface temperature, whereas because of the sea's transparency and thermal conductivity, the incoming solar radiation is dissipated through a large depth of water. Sea surface temperatures therefore do not vary as much during the day as do land surface temperatures. In order to generate a land breeze comparable in strength to a typical sea breeze there would have to be vigorous convection over the sea but not over the land. This could happen in conditions of a warm sea next to land cooling at night. In this way, useful land breezes can be generated in the tropics although it is rare elsewhere. However, yachtsmen should still be aware of land breezes as they may provide wind close inshore on nights which are completely calm further out to sea. Land breezes can sometimes be masked by katabatic winds which are large drainage flows of cold, dense air flowing down sloping terrain. Both of these phenomena may have a significant secondary effect if they interact with a larger scale onshore or along-shore wind to produce convergence or funnelling and hence stronger winds along the coastline.

Katabatic and Anabatic Winds

Katabatic winds, as previously mentioned, are those caused by cool, heavy air draining down a slope. Figure 27 illustrates their formation. They may appear similar to land breezes, but in fact the mechanisms that create katabatic winds and land breezes are completely different in that katabatic winds do not necessarily involve a complete circulation of wind with a reverse flow aloft. They are extremely local and variable, appearing to the sailor as strong, cold offshore winds. They can also occur inland wherever the right conditions of a sufficiently cool, steep slope are present. Glaciers and mountains in the northern hemisphere with north-facing slopes are frequently associated with katabatic winds.

The opposite of the katabatic wind is the anabatic wind, which is caused by air rising up a warm slope. Anabatic winds may be confused with sea breezes occurring along coastlines with south-facing hills or mountains.

Yachtsmen who are sailing in familiar waters will probably be aware of any local peculiarities, but a knowledge of katabatic and anabatic winds can be useful in explaining those winds that do not seem to match those of the forecast. It may be possible for a yachtsman to anticipate the wind regime in a new sailing area with complex terrain by looking at the local land contours and the direction of the steeper slopes and valleys.

Offshore Winds Near the Coast

The issue of changes to an offshore wind as it passes the coast is discussed in most books written for yachtsmen on sailing tactics, the wind or the weather. If the wind is onshore, a yachtsman standing on the shore may reasonably assume that the wind he feels is similar to that at sea. If the wind is offshore, this assumption is dubious as the wind is likely to alter as it

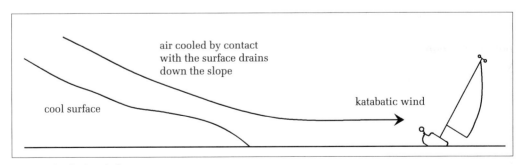

air cooled by contact with the surface drains down the slope

cool surface

katabatic wind

Fig. 27 Katabatic winds.

leaves the shoreline, that is to say, it may change both in direction and speed as the underlying surface becomes smoother and either warmer or cooler. It is also important since racing yachtsmen are always on the lookout for wind bends that may give a clue as to which tack is advantageous on a race course, and all yachtsmen are interested in how the wind will change as they approach a landfall.

There are two commonly held and frequently aired views regarding this. Some claim that an offshore wind bends to cross the coast more nearly at right angles and subsequently reverts to its previous course. However, possibly the most widely held belief is that, in the northern hemisphere, an offshore wind always veers clockwise out to sea.

The effects on an airstream crossing the coast are more complicated than may at first seem. Water surfaces are always less rough than land surfaces. They are also, generally, at different temperatures and this may have a significant effect on surface winds. For example, a cool sea will create a stable temperature profile. Stable temperature profiles produce more backing (in the northern hemisphere, veering in the southern) of the surface wind relative to that aloft than unstable ones, irrespective of surface roughness. Some limited information has been published in the scientific press concerning what really happens, but unfortunately it contradicts both of the commonly held beliefs among yachtsmen. What is probably the most thorough study was made in the late 1960s. This involved sifting through ten years of data from the coastguard station at Gorleston on the English east coast and Smiths Knoll Lightship situated some miles directly offshore from Gorleston. More than 3,000 occasions were found

when the recorded wind was offshore, and so the directions at the two locations could be compared. This dataset was the real wind that yachtsmen sailing offshore from the east coast would experience and it is equivalent to several lifetimes' worth of sailing experience. Overall, approximately as many occasions of backing as veering were observed. An interesting result emerged when the data was sorted according to whether the sea was warmer or cooler than the air (*see* Table 3).

For those occasions when the sea was warmer than the air by 6°F (about 3°C) or more, there was a mean veer of 7½ degrees. If the sea was cooler, then a mean backing of 5½ degrees was recorded. Whether this is useful or not is a moot point. Even if a yachtsman is aware of air–sea temperature differences, the variation in the published data is considerable, with a significant proportion of the recorded wind bends going in the opposite direction to the mean for the temperature contrast at the time. More recent studies have confirmed the link with temperature and have also shown large

Table 3

Results of a study of offshore winds at Gorleston on the east coast of England, from 1957 to 1966

	Mean Change in Wind Direction Offshore
On 738 occasions the sea was warmer than the air by 6°F (3.3°C) or more	veer of 7½°
On 659 occasions the sea was cooler than the air by 6°F (3.3°C) or more	back of 5½°

variability in the results. As well as this, they have demonstrated that refraction is not occurring and that winds can and do cross the coast at shallow angles.

There are innumerable complications affecting wind near a coastline, in particular the local terrain. For example, the presence of valleys running to the sea and gaps in coastal high ground can both have a huge effect on the wind up to a distance of many times the height of the terrain. This can result in significant effects several miles out to sea around the UK coastline which makes objective testing very difficult. It is also possible that the bending of wind by river valleys and estuaries has led to the notion of wind crossing the coast at right angles and then reverting to its previous direction. Another important factor is that air is not weightless. It has mass and momentum and therefore resists and reacts to changes over a period of time. Crossing the coastline upsets the balance of forces determining the wind direction and the wind readjusts gradually. Various levels of the atmosphere may react differently and may even overshoot and go into a sort of motion known by meteorologists as an inertial oscillation. Very little is understood about this and reliable theoretical models and detailed observations are both in short supply. The answer to the question 'How does the direction of an offshore wind change as it passes the coast?' seems to be that no-one can say for certain.

Coastal Convergence and Funnelling

In normal circumstances, the surface wind over land will be slower than that over the sea, so when an onshore wind hits the coastline, air at the surface will tend to accumulate or converge. Convergence is the term used by meteorologists to describe the situation when more air is entering a particular area than is leaving it. This has to be balanced by air rising or if the wind is not directly onshore its speed will increase along the coast. Another process can produce convergence if the wind is roughly along the coast. As a result of surface friction, the surface wind is backed relative to that higher up by an amount which is dependent on the surface roughness and temperature. This means that the surface wind over land is frequently backed relative to that offshore because of the greater surface roughness of the land. Figure 28 shows how this results in a band of convergence along the coast. This effect is dependent on the temperature structure over land and sea and is most likely when the sea is relatively warm.

Since convergence produces ascent as well as increasing wind speed, convergence zones are often marked by increased cloud development. The frontispiece shows a convergence zone along the north-east coast of the UK seen from a satellite. This occurred in the early morning when convection was present over a relatively warm sea and the land was still cool following a cold night. The surface wind was north-westerly and almost along the coast. The convection, visible as patches of large white cumulus cloud over the sea, is much enhanced along the coast where the surface wind trajectories are converging. Under this line of cloud the surface wind was probably stronger than ashore or further out to sea. There was little cloud over land at this time. Later in the day the convergence zone had disappeared, even though the wind direction was unchanged. The land had warmed and there

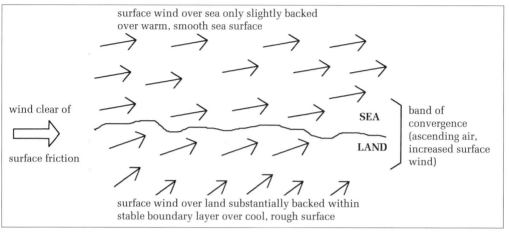

surface wind over sea only slightly backed over warm, smooth sea surface

wind clear of surface friction

SEA

LAND

band of convergence (ascending air, increased surface wind)

surface wind over land substantially backed within stable boundary layer over cool, rough surface

Fig. 28 Coastal convergence.

was little or no difference in wind direction over land and sea. Convective cloud was also occurring ashore. Predicting convergence zones, as in this example, is not a trivial business since it does require some knowledge of temperatures ashore and offshore. Nevertheless, it is a phenomenon to bear in mind when approaching a coastline from out at sea on days when conditions make convergence a possibility.

Divergence

The opposite of convergence is divergence. This occurs when more air at the surface leaves an area than enters it, causing air to descend from higher levels. Divergence produces bands along the coast that have reduced wind-speed and reduced cloud-cover. It is something to be aware of, but to the yachtsman is probably of less importance than convergence.

Convergence and divergence are phenomena that occur over a scale of tens or even hundreds of kilometres. On a smaller scale

the wind is influenced by the local terrain. The way in which wind is concentrated and increased in estuaries or channels surrounded by high ground is familiar to most people although the effect of even low-lying terrain, such as sandbanks or patches of marsh grass, can be surprisingly large. Bands of stronger wind caused by funnelling between obstacles are probably more familiar to inland sailors than those offshore and may provide local knowledge that is extremely useful.

Cliffs

The flow of air over cliffs often produces a characteristic pattern. Whether the cliffs are 10m or 100m high the flow pattern is usually similar in form. Figure 29 shows the typical patterns of flow away from a cliff (Fig. 29a) or into a cliff (Fig. 29b). It is impossible to give definite values for the size of the pattern as it is dependent on wind speed, direction and even the temperatures of the land, air and sea. The basic pattern is probably familiar to most yachtsmen, but a few features are worth emphasizing. The pattern shown is somewhat idealized and, in practice, regions where the wind is reversed will be unstable and marked by fluctuating and erratic wind. The distance offshore of the direction changes will vary over periods of several minutes. The lee eddy present for offshore winds is a well-known feature, but the bolster eddy, when the wind is blowing into a cliff, is less obvious. The implication for yachtsmen is to avoid getting too close to a steep lee shore if the wind is favourable further offshore.

Barriers

Barriers to wind near the surface need not necessarily be solid barriers such as brick

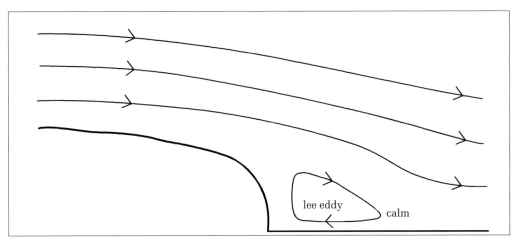

Fig. 29a Airflow downwind of a steep cliff.

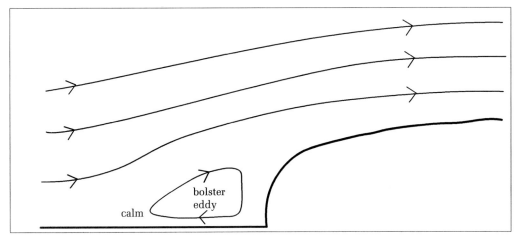

Fig. 29b Airflow upwind of a steep cliff.

walls. Lines of trees near a windward shore or fleets of yachts under sail will create barriers of varying density. A sufficiently solid barrier, such as a brick wall, is likely to produce a lee eddy behind it and a bolster eddy in front of it (Fig. 30a). Medium- or low-density barriers, such as lines of trees or closely packed yachts, can have very different effects (Fig. 30b). Figure 31 shows that though there is no lee eddy, the effects of the barrier can persist much further downwind. If, for example, the trees are 10m tall, then 100m downwind the wind speed will be 50 per cent of the free value; 100m downwind of a 10m high brick wall the speed will be about 80 per cent of the free value. This explains why medium-density windbreaks are more effective in protecting crops from wind. In fact, the bulk of the

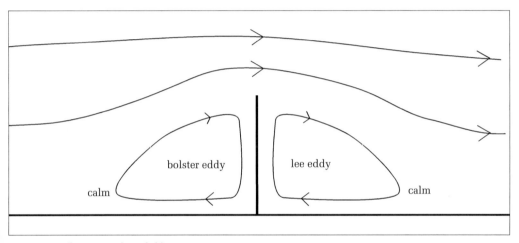

Fig. 30a Airflow around a solid barrier.

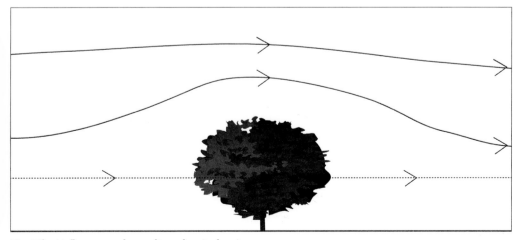

Fig. 30b Airflow around a medium-density barrier.

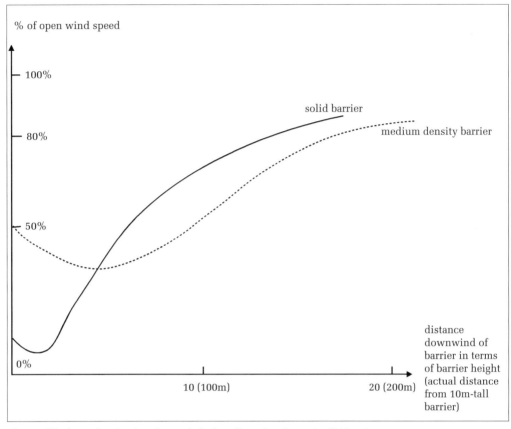

Fig. 31 Wind speed reduction downwind of medium-density and solid barriers.

research that has been carried out on wind barriers has been with agricultural applications in mind, although the results could also be useful to yachtsmen looking for wind or shelter from the wind. It is impossible to give hard and fast rules as the effects will vary considerably with wind speed, direction and barrier density. The yachtsman can only be aware of these effects and keep his eyes open for possible advantage. Figure 32 shows a plan view of wind flow around a medium-density barrier, in this case a tightly packed racing fleet approaching a downwind mark. This diagram is based on research on barriers that are used in agriculture and has not been tested by measurements afloat. It would be dangerous to apply it to yachts moving crosswind or upwind, although it will probably be reasonably accurate for yachts that are running downwind. It should be noted that the bulk of the yachts are in wind that is rather slower than the unobstructed wind speed. However, yachts just off to the sides of the pack are in a region of increased wind speed. The implications are obvious, that barriers can sometimes be used to advantage.

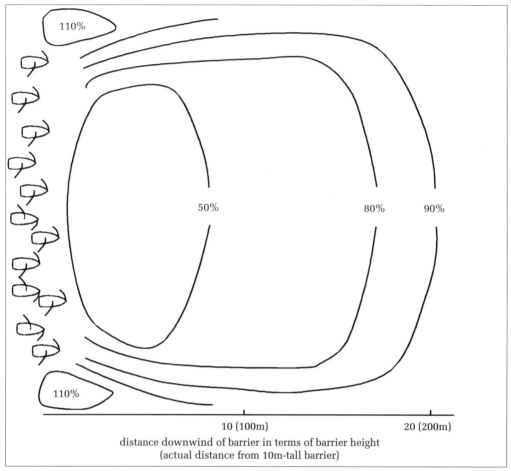

110%

50%   80%   90%

110%

10 (100m)   20 (200m)

distance downwind of barrier in terms of barrier height
(actual distance from 10m-tall barrier)

Fig. 32 Wind speed reduction downwind of a medium-density barrier (such as a closely packed fleet of yachts).

3

MORE ON WIND

Gusts

A gust is a short-term increase in wind speed over the mean wind speed. It is important to realize that wind speed variations occur over all time scales. Thus, at one extreme one hour may have a stronger mean wind than the next and at another extreme the wind may increase and decrease over a fraction of a second. A good demonstration of short-term wind fluctuation is provided by watching wind indicators on yachts in a crowded marina. Wind vanes only a couple of metres apart can be seen reacting differently, even moving in opposite directions as a gust passes. For many professional applications of wind data and forecasts, such as in aviation, the usual convention states that the mean wind is averaged over 10 minutes and the maximum gust is taken as being the highest 3-second average speed. The wind speeds broadcast in shipping forecasts and in reports from coastal stations refer to a 10-minute average, as does the Beaufort Scale (*see* Table 4). This convention is probably also appropriate to most small sailing craft. It should be recognized that descriptions of the wind as 'gusting force eight', for example, are meaningless, since a gale is defined as being an average speed over 10 minutes in excess of 34kt. Just because an anemometer reading has momentarily exceeded 34kt does not mean that a gale has occurred. In fact, in a typical force six (mean speed 22 to 27kt), gusts over 34kt are quite likely (*see* Table 4). There is a complication, however, in that gale warnings will be issued by the meteorological services if the forecaster expects gusts to exceed 43kt even when a mean wind speed over 34kt is not anticipated.

Gusts are due either to random turbulence resulting from friction and wind shear at the Earth's surface, or to the effects of convection currents in the atmosphere combining with the mean wind. The atmosphere at the surface is almost always turbulent to a greater or lesser degree. This produces a wind that will fluctuate in speed and direction in a system of turbulent eddies of various sizes. There is a relationship between the length of time that a gust lasts and its size. Rapid or short-lived changes occupy a smaller space than more prolonged changes, and as the Earth's surface is approached the predominant duration of fluctuations becomes less. For example, in a 10kt wind, at the middle of a 10m-high yacht sail, there will be a lot of wind fluctuations occurring over a period of a second or so. These represent eddies

Table 4

The Beaufort wind scale

Note: the range of gust speeds likely for each Beaufort force. These are not shown for values below force 3 because of the large range of gust factors at low mean speeds. The table also shows the equivalent terms used in land forecasts.

Beaufort Force	Description	Range of Wind Speeds at 10m Averaged over 10 Minutes in Knots	Approximate Likely Gust Speed in Knots	Land Forecast Description
0	Calm	less than 1		Calm
1	Light air	1 to 3		Light
2	Light breeze	4 to 6		Light
3	Gentle breeze	7 to 10		Light
4	Moderate breeze	11 to 16	14 to 22	Moderate
5	Fresh breeze	17 to 21	21 to 29	Fresh
6	Strong breeze	22 to 27	27 to 38	Strong
7	Near gale	28 to 33	34 to 46	Strong
8	Gale	34 to 40	41 to 56	Gale
9	Severe gale	41 to 47	49 to 65	
10	Storm	48 to 55	57 to 77	
11	Violent storm	56 to 63	67 upwards	
12	Hurricane force	64 upwards		

of a size similar to the size of the sail itself. This may be only of academic interest to most yachtsmen, although it should be of more concern to yacht designers and sailmakers. Yachtsmen, however, could benefit from some rules to help anticipate gusty conditions. The gustiness of the atmosphere is usually described by a term called the 'gust factor'. This is defined as the ratio of the maximum gust in a time period to the average wind. Sometimes meteorologists use a measure called the gustiness ratio based on the ratio of the range of wind speeds to the mean speed. The size of the gust factor depends to some extent on surface roughness. Over land, it will be larger than over the open sea and generally the rougher the surface the greater the gust factor. Over sea, 1.3 is typical but over rolling country, which could be relevant to sailors on estuaries or inland waters, about 1.7 is more likely.

Convection and Gusts

The description so far has concentrated on gusts resulting from friction-induced turbulence. Gusts originating from convection are generally longer than those due to turbulence, probably lasting 10 seconds or more. They are also usually more severe. These are a phenomenon of convective conditions and will occur when the air near the Earth's surface is sufficiently warmer than the air aloft to be buoyant. This air will then have a tendency to rise and so be replaced by descending cooler air from

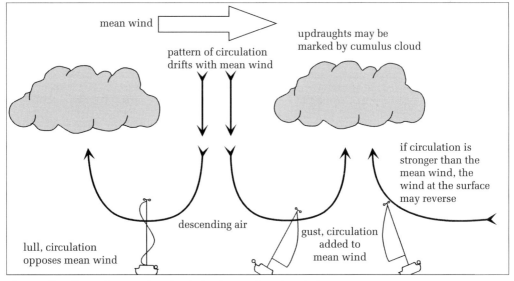

Fig. 33 The effects of convection circulation imposed on the wind.

above. The result is a larger scale of turbulence which may be organized into some sort of pattern. Figure 33 shows the basis of currents generated by convection. If the downdraughts are strong enough, for example if descending air has been cooled by precipitation, the gusts will be more severe and may strike the surface and spread out behind a 'gust front'. It is conditions of very strong convection that are usually responsible for the bizarre stories of showers of frogs, fishes and so on that occur from time to time. Strong updraughts may be accompanied by whirlwinds at the surface, drawing into the clouds small objects which will fall with any subsequent precipitation. During the yachting Olympics in Acapulco in 1968 one tropical shower was accompanied by a fall of live maggots which infested the covers of laid-up boats.

If the conditions are suitable, the currents are marked by clouds called cumulus clouds (*see* Fig. 9). On a large scale, convection in the atmosphere can produce a variety of patterns of currents and clouds. Cloud streets (*see* Fig. 9) may be visible from the surface but the more impressive patterns, known as open or closed cells, can really be appreciated from satellite photographs (*see*, for example, the frontispiece which was taken over the North Sea). However, whatever the large-scale pattern and regardless of whether clouds are visible or not, convection combining with the mean flow can produce gusts. The pattern of circulations driven by convection always drifts downwind. As an example (*see* Fig. 34), Yacht A is in a gust because the airflow from the circulation is adding to the wind, but yacht B is in a lull because the airflow is opposing the mean wind. It is possible for a reversal of the wind direction to occur if the airflow due to convection is greater than the mean wind speed. Thus, direction as well as speed can change in a gust. Note that in Fig. 34, yachts C and D experience gusts that back and veer respectively.

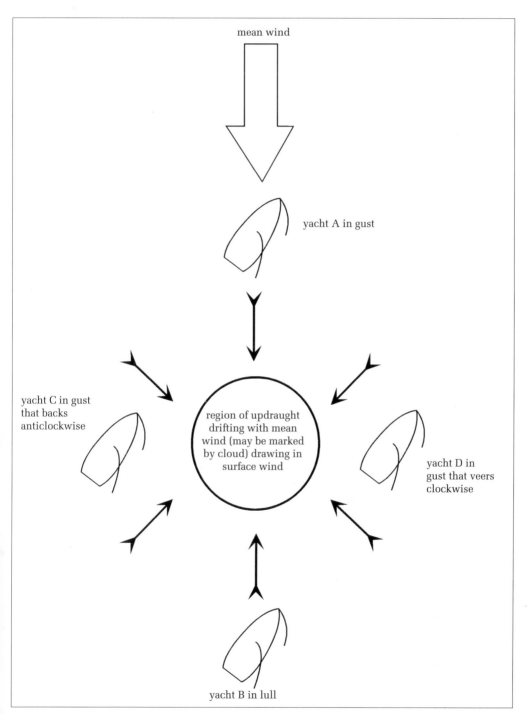

Fig. 34 A plan view around a region of updraught drifting with the mean wind.

There is a common belief amongst yachtsmen that wind veers (changes in a clockwise direction) in gusts. In the past, this idea had some support from meteorologists who favoured a model of gusts being wind brought to the surface from higher levels where it is generally stronger and is veered in direction (in the northern hemisphere), relative to the surface wind.

If the wind did veer in gusts it would be significant to many people. For this reason, the Meteorological Office has published several studies carried out under a variety of conditions aimed at finding out if there is any real effect. These all found no evidence for veering in gusts.

However, although there is no reliable tendency overall for wind to veer in gusts, it is always possible that on a specific occasion a yachtsman will experience a particular pattern of direction changes in gusts due to the effects of local terrain or particular cloud patterns. Some racing coaches set great store on the ability to identify and exploit such patterns, especially when the mean wind is very light.

Squalls

The term squall is applied only to severe increases in wind speed. Squalls are usually associated with some sort of larger-scale structure, such as a cold front or extensive convective cloud, and are generally longer lasting than most gusts and typically much bigger. Squalls associated with large downdraughts from convective cloud can be several kilometres across, while those accompanying the passage of a cold front can be up to tens of kilometres long.

A squall usually starts with an abrupt increase in speed followed by a gradual decrease. This means that a yachtsman may have little time to react by reefing sails or altering course. (This structure of sudden increase and gradual decline is often apparent even in gusts lasting only a few seconds.)

Studies of storm damage inland have shown the most extreme winds to be concentrated in bands a few hundred metres across. Records from yachts in the 1979 Fastnet storm have suggested similar effects at sea. Whilst some yachts in that storm experienced survival conditions, others, only a few nautical miles away, were making headway in much less severe conditions. Some crews showed remarkable dedication in recording pressure and wind data in their logs and this information has provided significant insights for both meteorologists and yachtsmen. Avoiding localized extreme winds is largely a matter of luck. Yachtsmen in the open ocean may be able to avoid the path of large cumulonimbus clouds by checking the bearings of the cloud in a similar manner to that employed when avoiding collisions with other vessels, albeit on a longer time scale. Likewise, the visible approach of heavy showers may give warning of strong downdraughts and consequent squalls. Perhaps the most useful advice that meteorologists can give yachtsmen is to be aware of the possibility of squalls and the conditions likely to produce them, so that they can be prepared.

Waterspouts

Some of the most violent winds at sea occur in waterspouts. These are the marine equivalent of tornadoes. In fact, a tornado crossing a lake becomes a waterspout for the duration of its passage across the water.

They are very local, sometimes only a few metres across, and are associated with extremely vigorous convection. Sometimes a distinction is made between 'true waterspouts' and 'fair weather waterspouts' which are much less violent. The latter may occur even with a cloudless sky and grow up from the surface rather than down from a cloud. In general, waterspouts are usually less violent than tornadoes. They are rare and the exact frequency of occurrence in British and European waters is difficult to judge. However, tornadoes occur in the United Kingdom on about fourteen days a year, although they are mostly minor outbreaks.

Tropical Revolving Storms

Tropical revolving storms are large features, typically several hundred kilometres in diameter. They are a particular kind of atmospheric feature differing from the frontal depressions of temperate or cool latitudes. Tropical revolving storms are created from conditions of unstable air overlying a warm sea with a sea surface temperature of at least 27°C. This situation is capable of supplying huge amounts of energy to the atmosphere by evaporation of water. When this subsequently condenses back to water, forming clouds and precipitation, it releases latent heat into the air. This results in massive updraughts over a large area which then cause more air to be drawn in from outside, evaporating yet more water from the sea. The process 'runs away' and results in strong winds into the centre of the developing system. The Coriolis effect causes the winds to rotate and the characteristic swirling pattern of strong winds, thick cloud and intense rain results. Tropical revolving

storms rotate in the same sense as depressions, that is anticlockwise in the northern hemisphere, but they do not have fronts and are generally smaller. There is usually a small area of lighter winds and little or no precipitation at the core or 'eye', although this area does experience very confused seas (see Fig. 35).

Tropical revolving storms follow more erratic routes than depressions and considerable forecasting effort is devoted to predicting their paths. If the mean wind speeds associated with a tropical revolving storm exceed 64kt then, in the North Atlantic or Western South Pacific, it is called a hurricane. In the Arabian Sea, Indian Ocean and around north-western Australia the same phenomenon is referred to as a cyclone whereas in the Western North Pacific they are called typhoons. Wind speeds in fully developed tropical revolving storms can reach over 100kt. Although the Beaufort Scale includes hurricane force twelve, and this is occasionally forecast or reported, this does not mean that a hurricane has occurred, only that the forecast or recorded wind, averaged over 10 minutes, exceeded 64kt. Britain has never experienced a true hurricane and is unlikely to do so unless something drastic happens to the global climate. Weather services sometime relate storms over Britain to old hurricanes, but all that has happened is that the remnants of an old hurricane have triggered the formation of a severe depression which in turn has affected the British Isles. The appearance of so many hurricanes in media forecasts is largely a result of the forecasters' skill in tracking individual features over long periods of time and distances.

Hurricanes cannot travel far inland, since they then lose their source of energy from the sea. Also, they cannot form on or

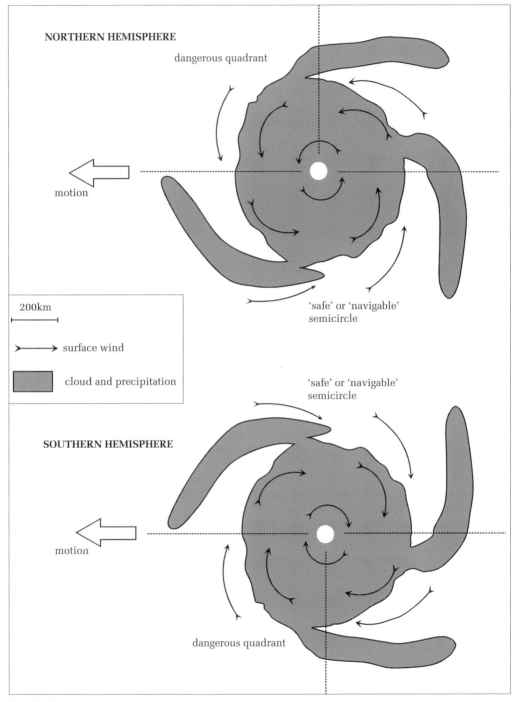

Fig. 35 Structure of a typical tropical revolving storm.

travel across the equator because, without the Coriolis effect, the winds and structure of a hurricane cannot be sustained. Neither of these facts is likely to be of much practical help to the yachtsman, although there is a lot of advice available to those who choose to sail in areas prone to hurricanes. The most important point is to take note of the time of year when hurricanes are likely to occur in that area and to pay attention to broadcast forecasts and warnings. Table 5 summarizes the times of year at which various hurricane-prone regions are most at risk.

In the absence of broadcast warnings the yachtsman should be aware of possible clues that may indicate the presence of a tropical revolving storm. A barometer is useful for predicting their presence but it must be in good working order. Using a barometer in the tropics is somewhat different to using one in temperate latitudes. Whilst the general variations in normal weather are much reduced in the tropics, there are daily variations in atmospheric pressure. These have a range of about 3hPa near to the equator, falling to 2hPa at 35 degrees. If, after allowing for this, the pressure is less than 3hPa below normal (as listed in the appropriate pilot book for the area), then there is a serious risk of a tropical revolving storm in the vicinity. Swell is also a good indicator of serious weather problems to come, since it can extend a thousand miles from the centre of a storm.

If a yacht is in the path of a hurricane the best advice to heed, if shelter is out of range, is to try to sail so as to be caught in the so-called 'safe' or navigable semi-circle. This is not actually safe at all and the word navigable may be based more on hope than expectation. The reason that this area is preferred is that a vessel forced downwind will be taken away from the direct path of the hurricane. The dangerous quadrant is to be avoided because its wind will pull boats into the hurricane's path. Within the hurricane itself it may be worth keeping on starboard tack (in the northern hemisphere), so that any progress will be away from the centre rather than towards it. The eye of a hurricane may indeed be calm, but having got into the eye where does a yacht go next?

In order to plan the best sailing and navigational tactics it is obviously essential that the yachtsman knows exactly where he is in relation to a tropical revolving storm. Ideally, he should make full use of all the warning services. If, however, he is in an area where broadcast forecasts are not available, then this could be an occasion when he benefits from using satellite imagery which is particularly good at showing up tropical revolving storms. Radio broadcasts from other yachts in the

Table 5

Frequencies and times of year of tropical revolving storms in the parts of the world most at risk

Location	Annual Frequencies 1958 to 1977	Time of Year at Risk
Western North Pacific	26.3	July to October
Eastern North Pacific	13.4	August to September
Western North Atlantic	8.8	August to October
Indian Ocean	18.7	January to March
Western South Pacific	5.9	January to March

region can also be extremely valuable, as can the interpretation of a number of other indicators. For example, Buys Ballot's Law may well be helpful. Its application will inform the yachtsman that when facing downwind, in the northern hemisphere, the centre of the storm will be somewhere to the left and slightly forwards (in the southern hemisphere it will be somewhere to the right and slightly forwards). If the storm is approaching then the atmospheric pressure will be falling. It should, however, be noted that tropical revolving storms do not have a consistent course and usually change direction at some time during their existence. They may eventually approach from any direction. In the northern hemisphere the wind will tend to veer in the dangerous quadrant and in the southern hemisphere it will back. The main difference in the recommended tactics, if one is caught in the dangerous quadrant as opposed to the safe semicircle, is to sail as close to the wind as possible in order to get far away from the direct path of the storm. If the yacht is in the direct path then running downwind may be the best ploy. It is worth bearing in mind that a modern yacht could well be sailing faster than a tropical revolving storm is moving and may actually overtake it. Some careful thought is always needed in assessing the true situation from a moving platform. Books written for deck officers on large ships often recommend heaving-to or stopping in order to assess the circumstances fully. If this seems excessively cautious during a race, then remember that these books are written for very powerful ships weighing thousands of tons sailing to tight commercial deadlines. Remember, also, that the full force of a hurricane, cyclone or typhoon can destroy any vessel ever launched (except for a submarine).

Wind Chill

Everyone knows from their own experiences that a strong wind feels much colder than calm air at the same temperature. Indeed, this difference can be dramatic. A crewman sitting dutifully on the weather rail may feel uncomfortably cold but on moving below decks, or just to a sheltered cockpit, he may suddenly feel hot and overdressed. This effect, whereby a stronger cold wind takes heat away from a person faster than a weaker wind or calm conditions at the same temperature, is referred to as wind chill. Sometimes the wind chill equivalent temperatures are quoted in forecasts, especially those aimed at the general public, and are generally derived from relationships called Steadman's Indices. These are based on experimental studies investigating the cooling effect of various combinations of wind speed and air temperature on exposed flesh. The resulting tables derived from these studies give the temperature that a wind of about 4½kt would need to give the same heat loss (or feel as cold) as the current conditions. For example, for a temperature of 0°C and a windspeed of Beaufort force eight, the wind chill equivalent temperature is −19°C. This means that a temperature of −19°C together with a wind speed of about 4½kt would give the same heat loss as 0°C in a force eight wind. Table 6 gives further examples.

This value of 'about 4½kt' may seem unusual, but is used for historical reasons. Originally, Steadman used miles per hour (mph) as his unit of wind speed and selected a round number of 5mph. This is equivalent to about 4½kt, which is roughly walking pace. Since individuals vary in their response to and their judgment of cold, and may also respond differently according to particular circumstances, the difference between miles per hour and knots may not be significant.

Although wind chill equivalent temperatures are widely quoted, they are also frequently misunderstood since they only apply to the rate of heat loss from exposed flesh which is being warmed metabolically. They are not, therefore, relevant to surfaces that are not being supplied with heat. For example, a thermometer exposed to the same wind as in the previous example would show the true temperature of 0°C and not the wind chill equivalent temperature of −19°C. In these conditions, frostbite, which requires tissue to be cooled below freezing, could not occur. As air moves faster, so heat is taken away more quickly from a body, but the body will never be cooled below the true air temperature. It is wind chill that allows us to cool hot food by blowing on it but, regardless of how energetically one blows, it will never be cooled below the temperature of one's breath. Despite these limitations, wind chill equivalent temperatures do have their uses as a guide to what sort of clothing to take for a day's outing or for a skipper who needs to make an inexperienced crew take foul weather seriously.

Weather on Tide

The weather can affect the tide level in two ways. Most obvious perhaps is the effect of surface atmospheric pressure. If this is low, then the tide will be slightly higher than predicted by the published tables; if it is high then the tide will be slightly lower than predicted. Published tide tables assume a pressure of 1,013hPa, which is a standard value used in many applications of marine and air transport. A pressure of 1,050hPa (unusually high but not unheard of) would lower sea level by about 0.3m, which though it sounds small could be significant. A much larger effect on tidal heights can result from the wind. If the wind blows in a particular direction for a length of time then the sea will tend to build up at downwind locations and consequently sea levels will fall at upwind locations. Although this effect can be larger it is much more difficult to estimate than the effect of pressure, especially in regions with complex tidal streams. Forecast services around the North Sea and in other regions where low-lying coasts are at risk from flooding devote a good deal of effort to forecasting the abnormally high tides which can result from the effects of weather. For yachtsmen, for whom too low a tide poses more of a danger than too high a tide, the moral of the story is to take the very accurate tidal predictions made in navigation classes a little less seriously and to allow a slightly greater margin of error in their estimation of tide heights.

Table 6

Approximate wind chill temperatures for various actual temperatures and winds

Actual Temperature	Force Three	Force Five	Force Eight
+10°C	+4°C	0°C	−3°C
+5°C	−2°C	−7°C	−11°C
0°C	−8°C	−14°C	−19°C
−5°C	−14°C	−21°C	−27°C

Too Hot – Too Cold; Weather and Health

It is generally well understood that extremes of weather can be bad for the health. Yachtsmen and women, in particular, can suffer from the effects of both high and low temperatures, even in temperate climates.

In high temperatures, sunburn and heat exhaustion can be very real hazards. In supposedly ideal sailing conditions of sun and wind together, a yachtsman can readily be exposed to high levels of ultra violet (UV) radiation without feeling any warning signs of overheating. In addition, a double dose of sunlight may be experienced because of reflections from the water's surface. Sunburn, in the short term, is both painful and embarrassing (some navies regard it as a self-inflicted injury and, therefore, a disciplinary matter). More seriously, excess exposure to UV radiation can lead to potentially life-threatening skin conditions. Whilst medical matters are beyond the scope of this book, it is worth emphasizing these risks since the industrial world has experienced a tenfold increase in skin cancers since the 1930s. This is commonly explained as being due to an increase in the population's exposure to sunshine. The medical profession's advice, to always protect the skin and eyes, should therefore be taken extremely seriously. There are, however, a couple of meteorological aspects to consider. Although clouds will attenuate the intensity of the most damaging UVB wavelengths, direct sunlight from a low solar elevation, for example at high altitudes in winter, will still be almost as intense as from a higher solar elevation. Note that the effects of the depletion of the ozone layer high above the earth, whilst extremely serious, are as yet of less significance to the spread of skin cancers than are changes in human behaviour. In fact, the natural day-to-day variations in the ozone layer over a mid-latitude location can be very large, possibly changing by 50 per cent or more over 24 hours, and this will significantly affect the levels of UV light at the earth's surface. The particular phenomena of global ozone depletion and the 'ozone holes' that are appearing over polar regions are very dangerous developments for many reasons. Curiously enough the publicity given to them may have an unexpected and desirable side effect in encouraging people to take sensible precautions when exposed to bright sunlight.

Heat exhaustion or dehydration are not necessarily confined to hot climates. It is not uncommon for a yachtsman, working hard in full foul-weather gear, to lose a lot of fluid as sweat and consequently overheat, even in relatively cool conditions. Drinks may not be so readily available as ashore, especially on smaller craft, so dehydration is a very real possibility.

Cold is also potentially hazardous. Yachtsmen exposed to cold winds are vulnerable to hypothermia, which results from excessive heat loss. The effects of wind chill are familiar to almost everyone. Similarly, most people are aware that wet clothes or skin can lose heat more rapidly than dry (this is something we all notice when getting out of the bath). The reason for this is that as the water evaporates it takes heat away from the skin or clothes. The lesson here, apart from the obvious one of keeping warm and dry, is that if someone becomes wet in cold conditions and it is not possible to change into dry clothing, then keeping the wind off them by getting them into shelter will offer some degree of protection. If this is not possible, then keeping on their water-proof clothing will slow down the heat loss from evaporation. The use of wet suits is a special case as these are designed to allow little transfer of water with the surroundings and so minimize any heat loss.

4

WIND AND WAVES

Formation of Wind-Waves

Waves are a vitally important part of the yachtsman's environment. Their size and speed can be critical to a yacht's performance and its crew's enjoyment. In their extreme form they can, of course, be dangerous.

The waves under discussion here are caused primarily by the action of the wind on the surface of the water, although sizeable waves can be formed by the effects of a very uneven seabed on a strong tidal stream even when no wind is present. By convention, waves that are the result of wind that has ceased to blow or that originate from distant winds are called swell, and waves resulting from the present wind are called wind-waves.

Obviously, the stronger the wind, the larger the waves. Equally obviously, waves will take time to respond to a change in wind speed. This introduces the concept of 'fetch', which is the distance over which a wave has developed. If the wind is offshore and a wave takes half an hour to reach a specified point offshore, then the waves can be no larger than could be produced by the wind in half an hour, even if the wind has in fact been blowing for a much longer period.

For a specified point further offshore, the wave will have taken one hour to travel from the shore and can therefore be larger. Therefore, increasing fetch increases wave height up to a limiting steady-state value. This is assuming, of course, that the wind has been blowing for some time. If the wind has only been blowing for half an hour then there will be no increase further out than the point reached in half an hour. Figure 36 shows waves building up downwind of a coastline and illustrates the preceding concepts.

The wind that is important to wave formation is the relative wind between the air and water. Thus, a 10kt wind blowing against a 1kt tide will produce the same waves as an 11kt wind blowing over stationary water. The same 10kt wind in the same direction as a 1kt tide will produce the waves appropriate to a 9kt wind over stationary water. We therefore find that a wind against tide effect, or an increase in wave height, will result as the tide turns against the wind. In reality, the effect of wind on waves is often much greater than can be accounted for by this simple model. Much larger changes are possible due to the effects of the seabed or tidal stream variations, which will be dealt with later.

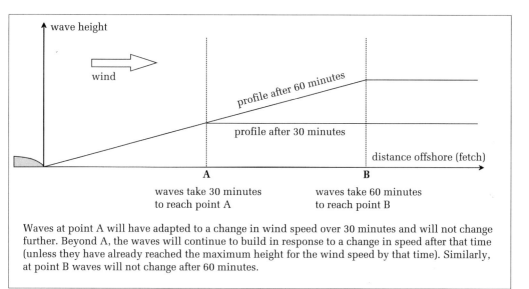

wave height

wind

profile after 60 minutes

profile after 30 minutes

distance offshore (fetch)

A

B

waves take 30 minutes
to reach point A

waves take 60 minutes
to reach point B

Waves at point A will have adapted to a change in wind speed over 30 minutes and will not change further. Beyond A, the waves will continue to build in response to a change in speed after that time (unless they have already reached the maximum height for the wind speed by that time). Similarly, at point B waves will not change after 60 minutes.

Fig. 36 Waves building downwind of a coastline.

The speed of wind-waves is closely related to the wavelength or period of the waves (the distance or time between the wave crests). As a rule of thumb, in deep water the speed of wind-waves in knots is three times the period in seconds. However, in water that is less than about half a wavelength deep the speed is reduced. This is why waves bunch up and break as they run onto a beach and accounts for some of the variations in wave height found over an area of sea with a shallow but varying depth.

Combinations of Wave Systems

In practice, waves affecting a given location are rarely simple. Usually there will be several overlapping wave systems. They will have originated from different wind directions and will have different speeds due to a changing wind field, and could be further complicated by one or more swell waves. Figure 37 shows how two wave systems overlap and combine to produce what are known as wave groups. Contributions coming from additional wave systems will modify the pattern still further, but the concept of a wave group still remains valid.

A curious feature of the wave group is that it moves at about half the speed of the separate wave systems that form it. Thus, waves appear at the back of the group, advance and grow through the group and then die away at its front. This explains why a wave upwind of a boat that appears threatening will often seem to die away mysteriously before it strikes. Similarly in a blow, an apparently small, innocuous wave advancing from windward can seem to grow suddenly larger and drench the occupants of the cockpit.

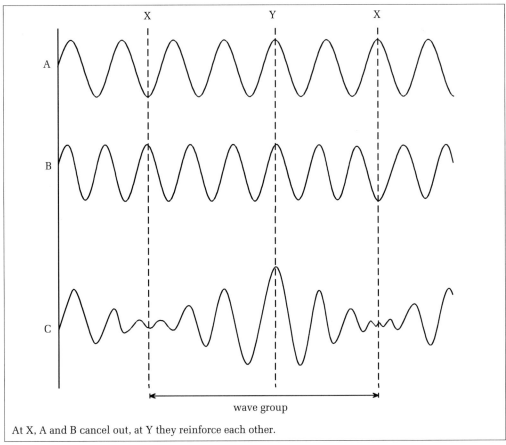

At X, A and B cancel out, at Y they reinforce each other.

Fig. 37 Interference patterns in waves. Wave systems A and B combine to produce the pattern of wave groups, C.

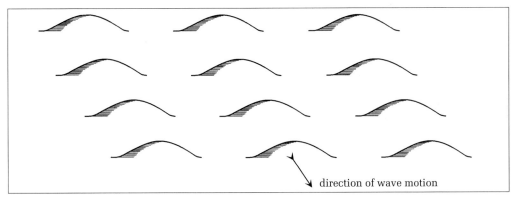

Fig. 38 A simple short-crested wave pattern resulting from two simple wave systems in slightly different directions.

Figure 37 also illustrates how the popular myth has arisen that the seventh (or ninth or fifth) wave is the largest. Obviously, patterns do occur, but they vary from time to time according to the particular wave systems that are combining together. In rough weather, it is often worthwhile looking out for the overall pattern of waves and wave groups so that tacking, gybing and other manoeuvres can all be carried out at a relatively calm moment. If wave systems moving in different directions are combining, then interference will occur in two dimensions. This will create what is known as a short-crested pattern (Fig. 38). The simple arrangement of long continuous wave crests of a constant height is called, logically enough, a long-crested pattern.

Waves in Shallow Water

We have already mentioned that wave speeds are reduced in shallow water. This has some important consequences. Figure 39 demonstrates waves running towards a beach at an angle. It can clearly be seen that the reduction in wave speed resulting from the decrease in water depth causes the direction of the wave to change, which leads to the commonly observed phenomenon of waves breaking on a beach nearly at right angles even though the waves offshore are approaching at a shallow angle to the beach. This phenomenon is called refraction and is similar in nature to the bending of light rays (light is an electromagnetic wave) by a lens or by water. This can

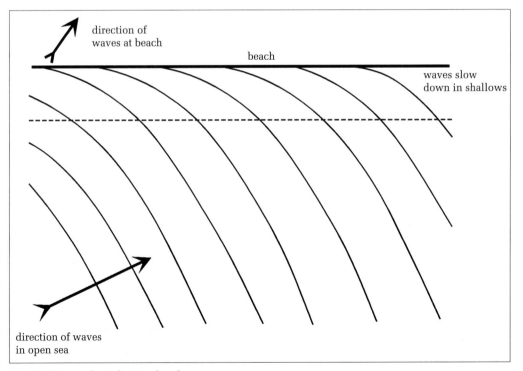

Fig. 39 Waves refracted onto a beach.

59

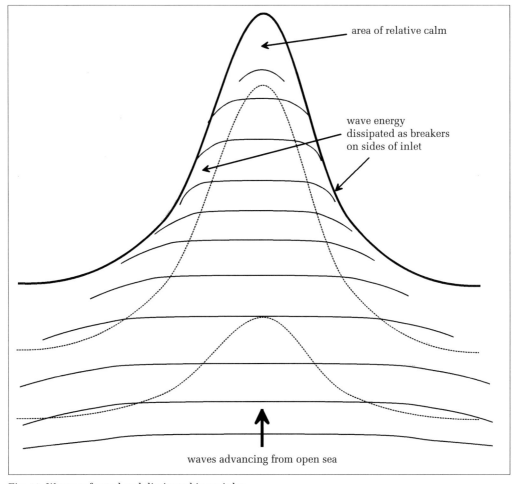

area of relative calm

wave energy
dissipated as breakers
on sides of inlet

waves advancing from open sea

Fig. 40 Waves refracted and dissipated in an inlet.

result in sea conditions being rougher or smoother than might be anticipated. Consider waves running into an inlet. We might expect the waves to grow towards the head of the inlet as it narrows, creating an uncomfortable anchorage. This is indeed the case if the sides of the inlet are steep. If, however, the sides slope gently then the waves will be refracted to the sides, causing the head of the inlet to be calmer (Fig. 40). Similarly, an island with shallow sloping edges can cause refraction, so that an area of rough sea will be found downwind where shelter might have been expected. Figure 41 shows the formation of a cross sea behind an island with sloping beaches. A shallow patch or sandbank below the surface can cause a similar effect.

Wind against Tide

When waves run from an area of relatively slack water into an opposing stream they

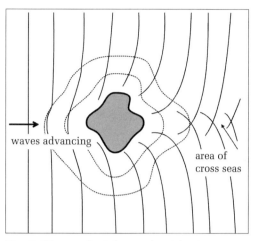

Fig. 41 Waves refracted around an island or sandbank with gentle contours.

will bunch up in a way similar to when they run into shallow water. Likewise, if waves run into a stream flowing in the same direction they will spread out. Thus tidal variations can cause effects very similar to the refraction discussed earlier. For example, if the inlet in Fig. 42 has a tidal stream running out of it then the stream will be stronger near to its centre than its edges. This could counteract any effects of refraction due to shallow water and produce the focusing effect shown in the diagram. This can result in a patch of rough water or cross seas at the entrance of an inlet during the ebb tide. The flood tide will, of course, produce the opposite result.

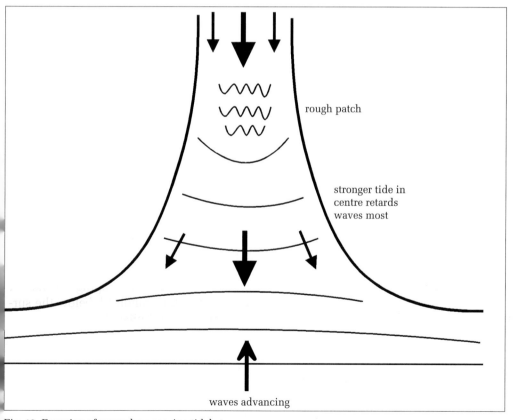

Fig. 42 Focusing of waves by a varying tidal stream.

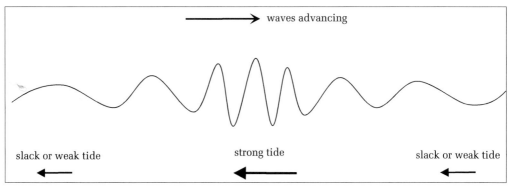

Fig. 43 Waves bunching up and growing in a region of strong adverse tide.

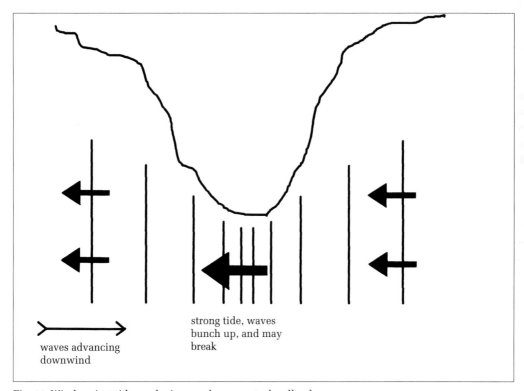

Fig. 44 Wind against tide producing rougher seas at a headland.

The effects of change in tidal stream can be dramatic. If waves run in to an opposing tidal stream they will bunch up and increase in height, creating a rougher sea. If the wave heights increase enough, the waves will begin to break. If the change in the current is large enough, then the wave cannot progress through it

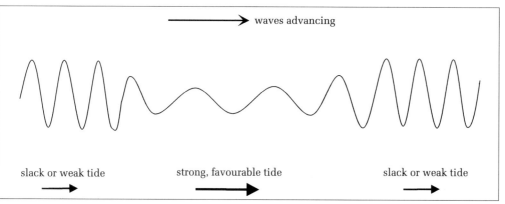

Fig. 45 Waves stretching out in a region of strong favourable tide.

at all and all its energy is dissipated as the waves break. A line of breakers, large or small, can often be seen marking an adverse tide. Figure 43 summarizes how an adverse current affects waves. This is why regions where the tidal stream accelerates, such as headlands or over sandbanks, show the most dramatic changes in sea state as the tide turns (Fig. 44). The same regions can sometimes be almost eerily calm when the tide flows with the wind. Figure 45 demonstrates how the waves are stretched out as they pass through the favourable tide. Only if the sea is shallow or the seabed very uneven will there still be a rougher sea around a headland when the tide flows with the wind. If waves break, much of their energy is dissipated. Therefore, if an adverse current around a headland or over a sandbank causes breaking then the waves downwind from it will not be as large as those upwind (see Fig. 46). This means that some areas of sea can actually be calmer in a wind-against-tide situation. It is important to remember that the most dramatic wind-against-tide situations are caused by changes in the tidal stream over short distances. If the sea as a whole changes speed, the effect on waves is small and mainly due to the change in relative velocity between the tide and wind.

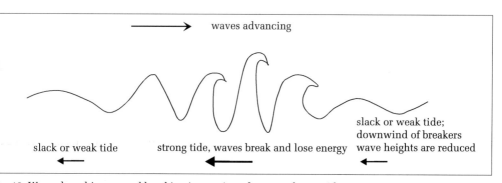

Fig. 46 Waves bunching up and breaking in a region of strong adverse tide.

The interaction of wind, waves, current and seabed is complex. Predicting wave conditions in advance requires either good local knowledge or very careful study and observation.

Waves and Rain

Many yachtsmen and other seafarers have long believed that heavy rain can calm a rough sea. Strange as it may seem, this piece of folklore is actually true, although the reasons for it are not completely clear.

Professional meteorologists have become interested in this phenomenon since the creation of weather satellites capable of utilizing radar to determine wave height and consequently wind speed over the oceans. Clearly, if the effect of rain is to reduce radar backscatter from waves, then wind speed will be underestimated in areas of rainfall. With this in mind, researchers at the University of Southampton have carried out experiments in wave tanks which have demonstrated the damping of waves by artificial rain. Similarly, scientists at the Goddard Space Flight in the United States of America have examined space-borne radar echoes from storms and have been able to correlate regions of low radar return signal with rainfall. The laboratory work suggests that the falling rain behaves in a similar fashion to an oil film, but the exact mechanism at work is not, as yet, fully understood. The fact that the laboratory experiments took place without any wind present shows that the folklore does not result from any hypothetical correlation between wind speed and precipitation intensity.

There may be practical uses for this piece of weather lore. The rainfall used in the laboratory experiments would be classified as heavy or violent if it was natural, and the space-borne radar data was taken from a severe storm. It may, therefore, take a good downpour to have a useful effect. On the other hand, the experiments showed that wave damping followed rainfall almost immediately. The implication is that if a yacht is being limited in its speed or pointing ability by waves, then a sudden shower can represent an opportunity to make more progress. Alternatively, if a yacht has been sailing in heavy rain a welcome rain clearance could have unwelcome side effects in the form of rougher seas.

5

WIND AND SAIL TRIMMING

True and Apparent Wind

The airflow over a yacht's sails depends not only on the true wind, but also on the motion of the vessel. If a yacht is stationary, the crew, sails and any wind instruments on board will feel and respond to the true wind blowing over the water. As soon as the yacht moves, it generates a flow of air relative to itself in the opposite direction and of the same speed as the speed of the boat. This flow of air, referred to as the boat wind, when added to the true wind, gives the apparent wind that will be felt by crew, sails and instruments. Figure 47 illustrates simple cases of yachts moving downwind, at 45 degrees and perpendicular to the true wind. In these examples, the

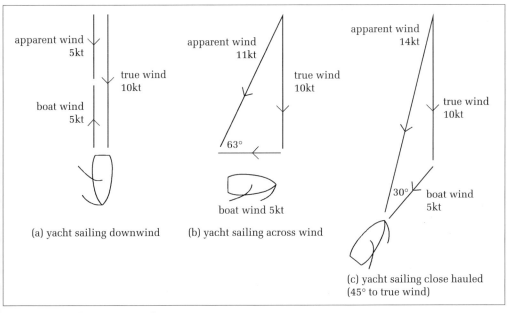

Fig. 47 True and apparent wind.

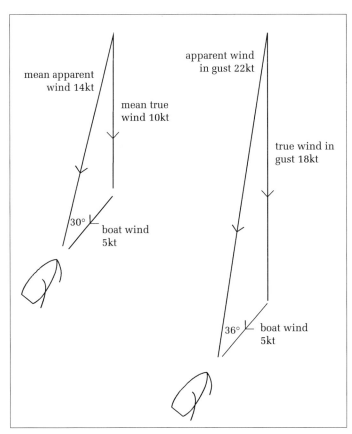

Fig. 48 More favourable apparent wind direction in a gust.

true wind is taken as 10kt and the boat's speed as 5kt. It can readily be seen that, for any direction other than directly downwind or upwind, the direction of the apparent wind is different to the direction of the true wind. Likewise, the wind felt by the yacht running downwind is 5kt and will feel to the crew as a force two wind would from a stationary position. On the yacht sailing close-hauled the crew will experience 14kt, similar to a force four wind from a stationary position. This demonstrates how difficult it can be to judge the true wind from a moving yacht. It can also be very difficult to ascertain to what extent a change in apparent wind is due to changes in the speed of the true wind or its direction, or indeed to a combination of the two.

The change in apparent wind direction with true wind speed is the main reason that an increase in true wind speed in a gust will often allow a yacht tacking upwind to sail a more desirable course. Figure 48 shows how an increase in true wind speed causes the apparent wind to move aft to a more favourable direction. In practice, the effect of a gust is complicated by changes in boat speed and consequently boat wind. A skilful helmsman will sail his yacht at an optimum angle to the apparent wind so that the yacht's course will also change. This will allow it to make better progress upwind in a gust.

Fig. 49 The effect of change in true wind speed on apparent wind direction.

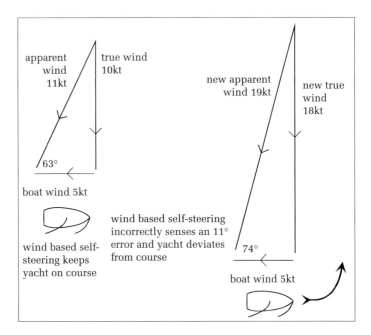

Figure 49 illustrates a yacht sailing under the control of an autopilot with a wind sensor or wind vane self-steering. The steering mechanism senses that the yacht is 11 degrees off-course after an increase in true wind speed to 18kt, and alters the rudder accordingly. Wind-based self-steering equipment can only set a course to the apparent wind and will alter course in response to a change in true wind speed, as well as to a change in true wind direction.

Lee-Bowing the Tide

A tidal stream or current can also generate an apparent wind. For example, if a yacht is stationary in the water in a 1kt tidal stream and there is no true wind, then the crew will feel a 1kt wind in the opposite direction to the stream. In general, the tide or current adds an extra component to any apparent wind. This tide-wind is added to the true wind and the boat wind to form the apparent wind that the boat will sail to. Figure 50 shows two examples of the effect of a 1kt tide on two yachts sailing on opposite tacks. The yacht on starboard tack has the apparent wind 26 degrees off the bow, but the one on port tack has the apparent wind 34 degrees off the bow and is, therefore, in a more favourable position. Generally speaking, a yacht with the tide or current on its lee-bow will gain an improvement in apparent wind direction from the stream. If the tide in Fig. 50 was reversed, then the yacht on starboard tack would have the tide on the lee-bow and consequently would have the advantage. This is why yachtsmen in tidal waters, or those sailing in rivers, are often advised to sail with the current on the lee-bow. All things being equal, this is good advice. An alert crew will be constantly appraising which tack is preferred in a given situation

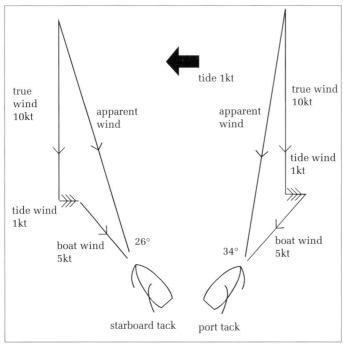

true
wind
10kt

apparent
wind

tide 1kt

apparent
wind

true wind
10kt

tide wind
1kt

tide wind
1kt

boat wind
5kt

26°

34°

boat wind
5kt

starboard tack

port tack

Fig. 50 'Lee-bowing the tide'. In this example, port tack is favoured as this yacht is sailing more free. In practice, it may not be obvious to the crew exactly what is happening, as they will perceive the wind referred to the water surface which moves with the tide. All crews will be aware that there is an advantage in 'going right' on an upwind beat. The real advantage in understanding 'lee-bowing the tide' is in being prepared for a change of tack being favoured as the tide turns.

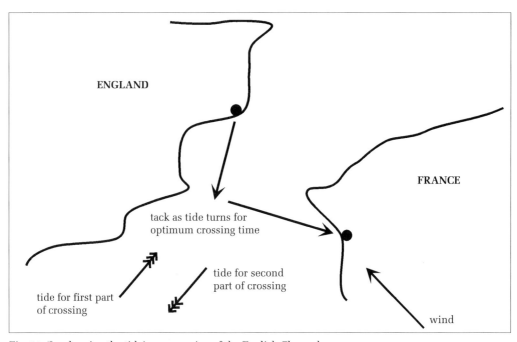

ENGLAND

FRANCE

tack as tide turns for
optimum crossing time

tide for second
part of crossing

tide for first part
of crossing

wind

Fig. 51 'Lee-bowing the tide' on a crossing of the English Channel.

and will therefore automatically take the tide into account. They may do this without realizing it because they will only be able to sense the wind relative to the moving water. However, tides turn and vary from place to place and a wise helmsman will always be prepared if a change in tide makes the opposite tack more attractive.

The classic application of this advice is in sailing across the English Channel against the wind. The best crossing time will be achieved by sailing on the tide-favoured tack until the tide turns and then tacking, so that the tide is on the lee-bow for most of the crossing (Fig. 51). In practice, there will be other factors for the skipper to consider, such as the need to hit a particular point on the opposite coast, anticipated wind changes during the crossing, avoidance of other vessels, and so on. Also, the wind will not often be blowing so closely from the direction of the destination that one tack is not much better than the other, whatever the tide is doing. There are even limits to the accuracy with which an Olympic course can be set to give an unbiased upwind leg. However, the general advice to lee-bow the tide does have merit and should be followed if it is relevant.

Wind Shear and Sail Twist

Near the surface of the sea, friction causes the wind speed to fall. The amount of change in wind speed over a yacht's mast will vary tremendously with meteorological conditions. Generally speaking, more change is likely in light winds or if the sea is relatively cool and the air is stable. For the purpose of illustrating the effects of this wind shear, we can take the wind at boom level for a typical cruising yacht as being about 60 per cent of that at the mast-head. Changes in true wind direction with height are probably negligible, except for extreme conditions or very tall rigs. This discussion is concerned with the average wind. At any instant the wind direction at the masthead could be as much as 10 degrees different from that at boom level as a result of wind turbulence. Figure 52 shows a run of wind recorded at Grafham Water, Cambridgeshire, UK. The sensors were situated at the water's edge and the onshore wind was about 18 to 20kt. The resultant trace is typical of the conditions afloat at that time. It illustrates the difference in direction between the wind at 6m and at 2m, roughly the heights of the masthead of a *Fireball*-class dinghy and the maximum chord of its sail. The key feature is the difference in direction that is sustained for appreciable lengths of time. For a few minutes, the direction at 6m is several degrees different to that lower down. The difference is not even consistent; sometimes the 6m wind is veered relative to that at 2m and sometimes it is backed. In practice, sails are trimmed to some sort of average wind and that is what we will consider next.

Figure 53a reveals how a change in true speed with height creates a change in apparent wind direction. There is a 13-degree difference in direction between the apparent winds at masthead and boom levels. This is the main reason why sails should be trimmed with an amount of twist. Distortion of the airflow by the vessel also occurs, but that effect is beyond the scope of this book.

In stronger winds, the amount of sail twist needed is reduced for two reasons. Firstly, the conditions when the true wind shear is largest are characterized by light winds, and, secondly, the relative effect of

Fig. 52 Differences between wind directions at 6m and 2m above the surface. The run of wind was recorded at Grafham Water in an onshore north-westerly wind of about force 5. Each plotted point represents a 10-second average. The main feature of interest is the periods of 10 to 30 minutes during which the wind direction at the two levels differs by several degrees.

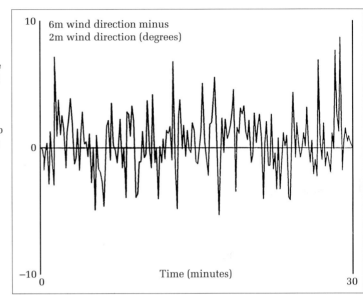

the boat wind is reduced at both masthead and boom levels. Figure 53b shows the variation in apparent wind direction if the true wind at masthead level is 18kt instead of 10kt and the percentage reduction to boom level is the same. The difference between masthead and deck is now reduced from 13 degrees to 8 degrees. This is why sail twist should be reduced in a gust or in stronger winds.

There is one more subtlety to apparent wind and sail twist, and that is the effect of tides or currents. Books written about sail trim or yacht tuning sometimes refer to occasions when different amounts of sail twist are needed on different tacks. This is often accounted for as being due to the change in direction of the true wind over the height of the mast. This could be the case inland or near the shore where the effects of complex terrain may generate a directional shear, or even offshore in extreme meteorological conditions, or for very tall rigs. Another possibility is the effect of a strong current or tidal stream on

the apparent wind. Figure 54 demonstrates how a tidal stream can cause a yacht to require more sail twist on port tack than on starboard. The difference is small, 14 degrees on port tack and 10 degrees on starboard, but it may be enough to be noticeable. Obviously, if the tide were reversed then more twist would be needed on starboard tack. Given enough time or distance, the wind profile will adjust to the current such that the wind direction, as measured by a boat moving with the tide, will not change with height. Then the sail twist will be symmetrical between tacks. However, tidal streams and currents vary with time and from place to place, so that in general the wind will not be in a local equilibrium with the water surface.

A note of caution must be added here. Throughout this chapter, typical values of wind speed, wind shear and so on have been used, but obviously the magnitude of the effects will vary according to the particular values on any given occasion.

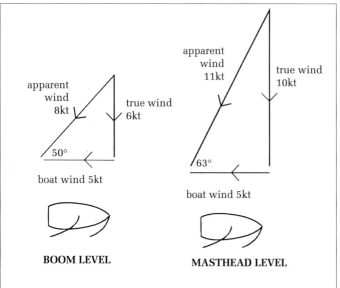

Fig. 53 Different apparent wind speed and direction at the masthead and at boom level.

Fig. 53a True wind 10kt at masthead (note 13-degree difference between apparent wind at masthead and boom level).

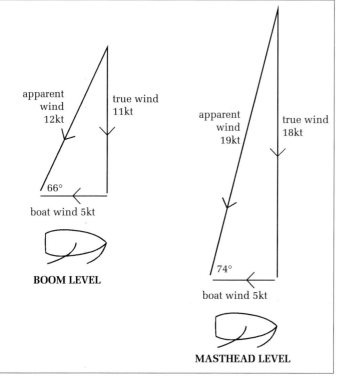

Fig. 53b True wind 18kt at masthead (note 8-degree difference between apparent wind at masthead and at boom level).

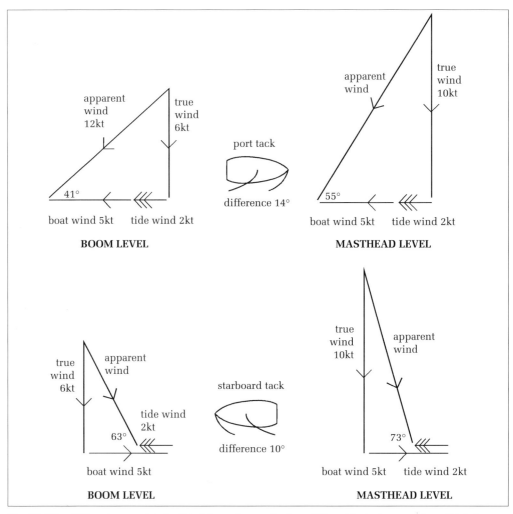

Fig. 54 Why different amounts of sail twist may be required on different tacks in currents or tidal streams. In this example, the tide effectively adds to the boat wind on port tack and reduces it on starboard. The opposite is also possible. The difference between 14 degrees of direction change over the sail on port tack and 10 degrees on starboard is small. It might, however, be detectable as a difference in sail twist required between tacks.

Also, the assumption has been made that conditions are more or less steady. In the real world, the surface wind is turbulent and constantly changing. Whilst the results in this chapter may help the yachtsman to anticipate how to sail his boat as efficiently as possible, there is no substitute for adaptability and careful sail trimming to the conditions present at the time.

6

VISIBILITY, FOG AND MIST

Definitions and Meaning of Visibility

Everyone is used to hearing broadcast reports and forecasts of visibility. Apart from the shipping forecast and other services aimed at seafarers, land forecasts are primarily concerned with visibility on the roads. Despite the apparent familiarity of this information it is not clear what the term visibility actually means. Visibility is usually taken by the layman as being the distance over which an object can be observed. A police officer producing a traffic report will presumably be basing his estimate on the distance over which the rear lights of a vehicle are visible. However, at sea things are not so straightforward, since different objects, such as small drab boats, brightly lit ferries, or navigation buoys, will be visible over different distances in the same atmosphere. Meteorologists define visibility as the distance over which the intensity of a beam of light is reduced to 5 per cent of its initial value. This quantity sounds complex, but is useful for two reasons. Firstly, it is equivalent to the distance over which the contrast between dark and light surfaces is reduced to 5 per cent, and a 5 per cent difference in

luminance is a good approximation of the threshold at which most people can detect a change. Secondly, it can be measured directly by simple instruments.

Night-time visibility is sometimes defined in vague terms such as the distance over which lights of reasonable brightness can be seen. Navigational charts give ranges of visibility over which particular lights can be viewed in good conditions. By convention, these are the distances at which the lights can be seen if the meteorological visibility is 10 nautical miles (nm). However, these figures should be treated with caution for a variety of reasons. Even though conditions may be good in the immediate vicinity of the yacht they may not be good all the way to the light source. A shower or patch of fog in between the yacht and the light, or a steady deterioration between them, can obscure a light that the crew of a yacht sailing in clear conditions would expect to see easily. Figure 55 shows how this may happen. This effect is also relevant to the interpretation of station reports in shipping forecasts. Some stations are manned and observers are trained to report the visibility as being the lowest in any direction, although at night they may not be aware of adjacent fog or showers. Automatic weather stations are equipped with sensors that measure the clarity of the air at the sensor site and use this to calculate an estimated visibility. In conditions of patchy fog or showers they may give unrealistically optimistic values, or if they are actually in a shower at the time of reporting, they may describe an unduly pessimistic value.

Most yachtsman's almanacs will give tables of distances to the horizon that can be used to determine whether a light will be in line of sight at a given distance from the relatively low viewpoint of a yacht cockpit. This assumes that light is travelling in straight lines. In practice, there will be a certain amount of refraction in the atmosphere. This means that rays of light will be bent slightly, either downwards or upwards. The amount and the direction of the bending varies with the temperature and humidity structure of the lower atmosphere. If the light is bent down-

wards, a light source may be visible even though it should be hidden by the curvature of the Earth (*see* Fig. 56a). Likewise, if the light is bent upwards, a light source may not be visible even though the air is clear and it should be in line of sight (*see* Fig. 56b). The phenomenon of refraction may also affect radar and sound waves. The effect on radar is unlikely to be significant to seafarers, other than crews of warships using long-range radar to detect an enemy, but refraction of sound can cause foghorns to be audible at greater distances and yet inaudible at much closer range.

There are occasions when bright lights that are varying in a regular manner, such as those emanating from lighthouses or lightships, can be picked up at greater distances, despite being below the horizon, by observation of the light scattered by low cloud (*see* Fig. 57). What is actually observed is called the loom of the light,

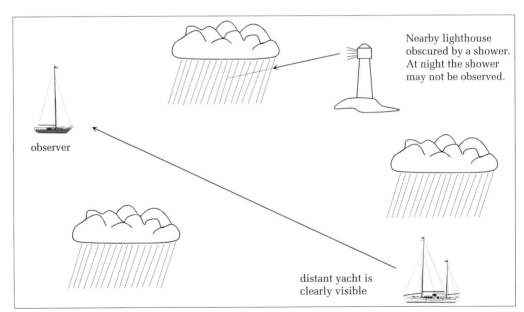

Fig. 55 Clear conditions around a yacht and good visibility to distant objects does not always mean that navigational marks are clear.

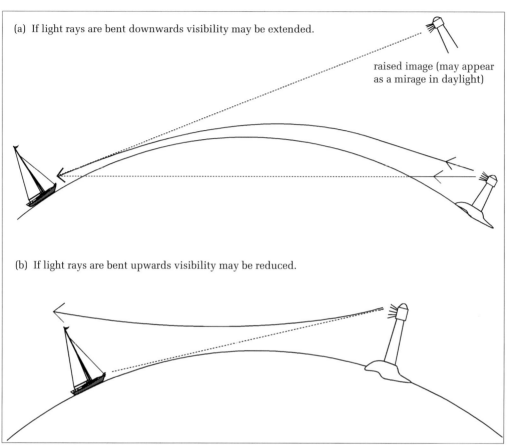

(a) If light rays are bent downwards visibility may be extended.

raised image (may appear as a mirage in daylight)

(b) If light rays are bent upwards visibility may be reduced.

Fig. 56 Refraction of light rays can make distant objects visible despite the curvature of the earth (a) or reduce the range of visibility (b).

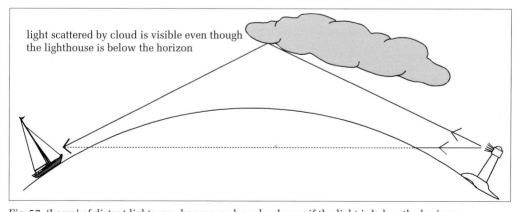

light scattered by cloud is visible even though the lighthouse is below the horizon

Fig. 57 'Loom' of distant lights may be seen on low cloud even if the light is below the horizon.

and while it will not be enough for a navigational fix, it can be of some reassurance to a crew regarding their approximate position and the real visibility. There can be some risk, however, in using the loom of a light to obtain a rough fix since cloud cover can be very uneven and there is no guarantee that the loom will match the direction of the light source.

Types of Fog and their Formation

Fog forms when moist air is cooled. In order to understand the mechanism by which this occurs, the concept of dew-point temperature needs to be appreciated. Warm air can support more water vapour suspended in it as a gas, than can cool air. This means that as moist air cools, a point is reached when it is no longer capable of supporting all the water vapour it contains. At this point, the dew-point temperature, water vapour will start to condense out as a liquid forming tiny droplets of water in the air which become fog, mist or cloud. Water vapour itself is a transparent gas but the droplets of water will scatter light, which in turn will affect the transmission of light and so reduce visibility. Water vapour will form water droplets, rather than ice, at temperatures well below freezing, and so ice fogs, formed by large concentrations of ice particles, are only found at temperatures of about −20°C or below. When land forecasts refer to freezing fog they do not mean that the fog itself is made of ice particles, but that surfaces, such as roads, are likely to be below freezing and so the fog will leave ice, rather than water, on any surface with which it comes into contact.

Air is cooled below its dew-point temperature primarily by contact with an underlying surface of land or water that is below the dew-point. This can occur in two ways to produce types of fog significant to yachtsmen.

Radiation Fog

Radiation fog forms over land on cloudless nights. The Earth's surface cools because the loss of energy by emission of infra-red radiation is not balanced by downward emissions from the air and cloud above or energy from below ground. However, when the surface has cooled below the dew-point, fog is not necessarily a foregone conclusion. If there is no wind, the water vapour will condense out as dew or frost and no fog will form. If the wind is too strong, turbulent mixing will spread the cooling over such a depth of atmosphere that the air does not itself cool below the dew-point before dawn. Although radiation fog does not form at sea it can drift out to sea to affect coastal regions (forecasts may refer to coastal fog patches), and may obscure coastal lights or landmarks.

Advection Fog

Of greater seriousness to seafarers is the second type of fog, known as advection fog. Advection is the term used by meteorologists to describe the movement of air with some particular characteristic. In the case of advection fog, air with a relatively high dewpoint and temperature is carried over a cooler surface. The air is cooled by the underlying surface and when it reaches the dew-point temperature, fog forms. This kind of fog is sometimes called sea fog and has a variety of local names, such as Haar

Water Vapour in the Atmosphere

The concept of 'dew-point' is essential to the understanding of fog and cloud formation. The basic concept of a temperature below which water vapour condenses out of the atmosphere is straightforward enough and is all the yachtsman really needs to understand. However, the physics behind the concept of dew-point and the processes of condensation are subtle and may be of interest to those more curious about meteorology. Water vapour is a gas, which means that its molecules are in free motion and will consequently mix with the other gases in the atmosphere such as oxygen, nitrogen and so on. Molecules of water vapour are actually lighter than most other molecules in the atmosphere yet take up the same volume. Perhaps rather surprisingly, this means that moist air is lighter than dry air. In liquid form as opposed to gaseous form, water molecules have less energy and are in physical contact with each other.

If a surface of water is in contact with air two processes occur simultaneously. Firstly, molecules of water that strike the surface may 'stick' and join the liquid rather than bounce off it. Secondly, molecules in the liquid, with above average energy, may break free and join the water vapour molecules in the air. This second process, in particular, is extremely temperature-dependent. At higher temperatures more liquid molecules will have sufficient energy to break free from the attraction of their neighbours. This means that for any temperature there is a certain concentration of water vapour (known as saturated vapour pressure), at which these processes are in balance and as many water molecules will be lost to the air as are gained from it. The vapour pressure of this equilibrium state is greater at higher temperatures.

In normal circumstances the actual concentration of water vapour in the air is less than saturated (saturated air being air that is holding the maximum possible quantity of water vapour), and a water surface will evaporate. In doing so, it will slowly lose water molecules to the air above. If, however, the concentration of water vapour in the air is greater than saturated then a water surface will gain molecules from the air. If a sample of air, less than saturated, is cooled below a critical temperature then a free water surface will gain water molecules faster than it will lose them. This is because too few of the water molecules will have enough energy to break free from the water's surface. This critical temperature is the dew point. The dew point is the temperature at which a particular mass of air will start to release water spontaneously as dew, fog or cloud. However, some sort of suitable surface must initially exist for this to occur. This may be the surface of the Earth for the formation of dew, or so-called condensation nuclei in the air for the formation of fog. In practice, condensation nuclei, such as tiny particles of salt, are nearly always present in the air to enable these water droplets to form. If no such surface exists then dew, fog or cloud cannot form and so when the temperature falls below the dew point the air is said to become supersaturated. In reality, because of the usual presence of condensation nuclei this is a very rare occurrence. Once tiny droplets have formed on condensation nuclei then these droplets themselves are very efficient at collecting water molecules as the air cools further.

or Fret. Unlike radiation fog, it can accompany strong winds and may persist for several days. Since it needs the combination of warm, moist air and cool sea it usually occurs in late spring when the air–sea temperature contrast is at its greatest. The seas around the north-east coast of Britain are especially susceptible to this phenomenon. Sea fog will clear rapidly with the arrival of low dew-point air, for example after the passage of a cold front.

Visibility Reduction by Precipitation

The effects of precipitation on visibility, especially in showers, can be dramatic. Significant reductions are possible with even light rain, and heavy showers or snow can change clear conditions into poor visibility almost instantaneously. Ironically, the meteorological conditions that produce showers are also likely to give very clear air in between so that the element of surprise that a sudden shower can cause is much greater. At night, there may be few visual clues to warn of imminent showers. A helmsman or navigator sailing under a night sky full of stars is well advised to look out for cloud development if he or she has reason to think that showers are possible. Showers need not be a problem to the yacht itself, but the sudden disappearance of a nearby ferry or fleet of trawlers because of an intervening shower can be quite disconcerting. The deterioration in visibility due to fog or the onset of steady rain or snow may be unwelcome but will not come as a surprise.

7

THUNDERSTORMS AND LIGHTNING

The Theory of Lightning Formation

One of the advantages of meteorology over most other sciences is that so many of its various phenomena and processes are visible to everyone. This is particularly obvious in a thunderstorm, during which lightning makes an impressive display for the meteorologist and layman alike. Such a display can also be a little unnerving, especially if it is being viewed from an isolated yacht with a tall metal mast pointing up towards the clouds. In fact, the risk of a lightning strike in these circumstances is not as great as it might appear for reasons that will be explained later.

Whilst the basic physics of a normal lightning stroke has been fairly well explained, the process by which a cloud accumulates electric charge is not, as yet, completely understood. Meteorologists have established that lightning occurs only after a cloud has developed to such a height that its structure passes through the freezing level, that is, the level at which the air temperature has fallen to 0°C. Lightning is most likely when the cloud-top temperatures are less than −20°C. It is sometimes possible to anticipate this from

simple cloud observations. Even if the weather seems fine, the presence of clouds like those shown in Fig. 58 can warn of trouble to come. They are similar in many ways to the familiar cumulus clouds that form within a few thousand feet of the surface as a result of vertical air currents, except that they are found at much higher altitudes. Such cloud formations indicate that the atmosphere at about 10,000 to 15,000ft (3,000 to 4,500m) can support vertical cloud development. This means that, once it has formed near the surface, a cloud can grow to a sufficient height to create a lightning risk. These clouds are known by meteorologists as altocumulus castellanus. Sadly, there does not seem to be a simpler name.

Thunderstorms themselves are particularly associated with the kind of cloud shown previously in Fig. 10. These clouds are known as cumulonimbus and may extend over 30,000ft (9,000m) into the air from a base of a few thousand feet or less. The characteristic fibrous anvil at the top of these clouds is composed of ice crystals. These only develop when the temperature of the cloud droplets is about −20°C to −40°C. Above this temperature, cloud droplets can remain as supercooled water by virtue of their tiny size. The presence of

Fig. 58 Altocumulus castellanus. These clouds are sometimes a precursor of thundery conditions.

a mixture of ice and water and the formation of precipitation is apparently critical to cloud electrification. Meteorologists have shown that when droplets of super-cooled water freeze onto falling hailstones they may shatter, resulting in ice splinters and hailstones carrying opposite electrical charges. These splinters of ice are more easily carried to the top of the cloud by updraughts within it than are the hailstones. This will effectively generate an electric current, which in turn will create different electrical charges at varying heights throughout the cloud. Because the hailstones may melt into rain before reaching the ground, this process can occur even if no hail is observed. Although a complete answer is still some way off, at least some possible mechanisms for creating electrical charge in a cloud have been established.

Once the charge distribution has created a powerful enough electric field, a lightning stroke occurs. This may be within the cloud, causing so-called sheet lightning, or from the cloud to the ground, causing forked lightning. Virtually nothing is known with certainty about the more obscure forms of lightning such as ball lightning or the upward flashes from the tops of clouds which were first reported in the 1920s. These are now known as 'sprites' due to their appearance when viewed from spacecraft. If lightning is occurring out of sight and hearing it may still be picked up as distinct 'clicks' on radio at long-wave frequencies. The release of radio energy in a thunderstorm at long wavelengths can disrupt navigation systems, such as Loran C, which uses similar wavelengths. Global positioning systems (GPS) are much more resistant because they use much shorter wavelengths.

Lightning Risk

Although a yacht's metal mast and rigging are often the tallest objects around in a thunderstorm at sea, they are rarely struck by lightning. This may seem strange, but it is due to the nature of a lightning strike (see the process shown in Fig. 59). Initially, a relatively weak current flowing down a 'stepped leader' travels down from the base of the cloud in a more or less random sequence of steps. This continues until it is within a short distance of the surface, usually about 10 to 15m, though this can vary considerably. In this context, the surface includes a yacht's mast or rigging. This process is shown in Figs 59a to 59c. The main discharge then follows from the surface upwards and it is this return stroke which carries the main current in the strike. There may be several return strokes, each preceded by a leader. The entire process lasts less than a second, but the sequence of separate strokes may cause a visible flickering of the flash. Figure 59d shows a return stroke connecting with the leader at its nearest approach to the surface. The yacht in these diagrams appears to have experienced a lucky near miss simply because the random path of the leader stroke never came closer to the mast than it was to the sea. On land, even a near miss can be very dangerous as the strike can generate extreme-ly high voltages along the ground. At sea, the high conductivity of the water dramatically reduces this effect.

There is little that can be done to reduce the chances of a lightning strike at sea. If the leader stroke happens to approach the yacht's mast before the sea's surface then the yacht will surely be struck. There is no evidence for the notion that electrically connecting a yacht's mast to earth increases the risk of a strike. The best practice is to ensure that a yacht has a suitable path for a lightning stroke to take without causing serious damage. This involves the same procedures that would be involved in installing a lightning conductor ashore. A length of thick wire between the mast and a suitable metal area below the waterline may suffice, but the cable must be substantial and all connections electrically sound. Some yacht builders do install lightning protection as standard. When the world's navies and trading fleets were based on wooden ships with wooden masts and rope rigging, lightning sometimes caused serious casualties. Early efforts to provide protection involved hoisting long, thin chains aloft in storms and dangling the ends in the sea. This was fine in theory but clumsy in practice, and sailors were occasionally electrocuted in the process of hoisting the chains. The solution finally chosen was an arrangement of copper strips down a mast connecting to a metal plate below the waterline. The top of the strip should end at the highest point above the waterline and some sort of lightning rod or spike may be needed. Contrary to popular belief, the end of this spike need not be pointed. All that really matters is that the metal is closer than any other metal on the yacht to the end of any stepped leader that approaches.

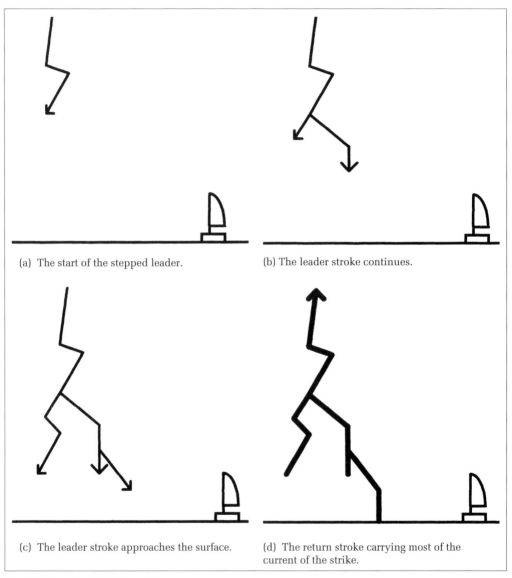

(a) The start of the stepped leader.

(b) The leader stroke continues.

(c) The leader stroke approaches the surface.

(d) The return stroke carrying most of the current of the strike.

Fig. 59 Stages in a lightning strike.

Thunder

The sound of thunder results from the rapid expansion of air along the path of the lightning stroke as it is abruptly heated to a temperature rather greater than that at the surface of the sun. Thunder lasts for a relatively long time after the momentary stroke because the sounds from the different parts of the stroke take different times to reach the listener. This can be illustrated with an extreme case. Suppose a stroke of lightning starts in a cloud 1,000m directly above and hits the ground a few metres away from you. At a speed of 300m per second or thereabouts the sound from the start point in the cloud will be audible for more than 3 seconds after the initial flash and bang, although in this particular case you might not be paying much attention!

Other Hazards of Thunderstorms

Thunderstorms or more accurately the kind of clouds that are associated with them, can produce two other forms of hazard.

Deep cumulus or cumulonimbus clouds contain very strong updraughts and downdraughts. The downdraughts can strike the surface and spread out in the form of vicious squalls. These can strike a yacht from a direction that is very different from the prevailing wind direction.

The other hazard comes from the heavy precipitation associated with thunderstorms. This is dangerous because it may result in sudden, dramatic reductions in visibility, which can be all the more hazardous because they will be occurring in conditions of generally good visibility and may cause the unexpected disappearance of navigational marks or an approaching ship.

St Elmo's Fire

One of the most spectacular of meteorological phenomena is St Elmo's Fire, named after the patron saint of Mediterranean sailors. It takes the form of luminous blue or red 'flames', up to about 10cm (4in) long, that appear around the extremities of a vessel's masts or spars. Sometimes they may even form on boat hooks held in the hands of sailors. Mountaineers climbing in thunderstorms have been known to see it on their fingers and heads. Often there is an accompanying hissing or crackling sound. St Elmo's Fire occurs during, or more usually just before, thunderstorms. It results from a steady flow of charge from the ground due to the large voltage gradient, or electric field, in the atmosphere at the time. It is an electrical, atmospheric phenomenon which is quite harmless but which can be extremely unsettling to a crew. Strangely enough, St Elmo's Fire used to be regarded as a good omen since sailors of old believed that the thunder and lightning it foretold was an indicator of the end of the storm.

St Elmo's Fire is most noticeable around pointed objects as these tend to concentrate the electrical field. Possibly this has reinforced the view that lightning conductors should be pointed. There seem to be two theories as to why this should be so. One is that the increased discharge that occurs with a pointed object in some way reduces the chance of a lightning strike by influencing the clouds above, or by reducing the voltage gradient. The other is that the stream of charges increases the effective height of a lightning conductor thereby increasing the area of protection it offers. Neither of these ideas is universally accepted, although lightning conductors are usually pointed. Some lightning conductors have even been designed to generate a stream of charged particles by the use of piezo-electric crystals or radioactive material, effectively creating their own form of St Elmo's Fire.

St Elmo's Fire can also be seen on occasion around the wing tips or antennae of aircraft. Streamers up to 4m (13ft) long have been reported. Aircraft, being electrically isolated, are vulnerable to the build up of static charge. They are usually equipped with arrays of pointed wires so that the charge can be lost more quickly and these will be the main points from which St Elmo's Fire will grow.

8

FORECASTS

Services Available

Since there are an enormous number of weather forecast information services available, the details of which vary considerably from year to year, the reader is strongly advised to consult the almanacs and annual publications available for up-to-date information. However, although a detailed analysis would be impractical here, it is possible to describe the advantages and disadvantages of various categories of forecast service.

National Radio Broadcast (Shipping Forecast, Inshore Waters Forecast)

These forecasts are specifically intended for yachtsmen and other seafarers. They provide good background forecasts for periods of about 24 hours.

Local Radio Forecasts Targeted at Yachtsmen

The forecasts that are broadcast on local radio will sometimes provide more local detail. They may also be transmitted more regularly than those of the national broadcasts.

Radio Land Forecasts

These do not necessarily have the detail of a targeted forecast but can still be very useful. For instance, they will often mention sea breezes along coasts in cases when the main shipping forecast ignores them. They will also frequently provide a guide to weather extending over the next few days rather than just the next 24 hours.

Marine Radio (VHF and MF)

Weather information is broadcast regularly on appropriate channels from coastguard and other stations. Apart from broadcasts at preset times, weather warnings will also be issued as necessary. The broadcast may be a repeat of the forecasts available elsewhere, or may be greatly enhanced by real-time observations from a coastguard.

Weather information may be available, in principle, on request from coastguard stations. However, the density of radio traffic is constantly increasing and it is unreasonable for a yachtsman to expect to be able to call a busy coastguard station for a forecast simply because he was too inefficient to obtain the information elsewhere. There are also commercial constraints that in future may make coastguards unable or unwilling to supply anything other than pre-arranged broadcasts and warnings.

Telephone and Facsimile Services

There are a number of organizations offering weather information by telephone or facsimile. The service is available at all times and the use of facsimile provides the information as hard-copy text or charts. There is, of course, a fee to be paid for these services, and whether or not the fee is reasonable is a matter of judgment and debate. However, no-one is forced to use these services, and it is not clear that yachtsmen should expect their sport to be subsidized by others.

Newspapers

Weather forecasts in newspapers are generally very basic, although some quality newspapers print weather charts which include major features such as isobars and fronts. The charts are small, but still of some use to a yachtsman who wants a general picture of what is happening to the weather.

Television

Visual presentation of a weather forecast, especially in colour, is very effective.

Television-Based Information Services (CEEFAX, ORACLE, and so on)

The presentation in these media is generally not as good as a broadcast television forecast, but the information is available at any time. Especially useful to the yachtsman is the shipping forecast. It is easier to assimilate in this form than the radio broadcast version.

Internet

The Internet is a means of data-exchange that is growing extremely rapidly. There is an overwhelming variety of information available for those with the equipment to receive it and who know where to find it. Significantly, the Internet is a source that is not restricted to particular times of broadcast. It can also provide hard copy of text and charts. Satellite imagery is also available on the Internet for those yachtsmen capable of interpreting it.

Navtex

Navtex is a system transmitting important navigational data, including weather information, in text form. The broadcast frequency is 518kHz (kiloHertz), and the range of the system is about 300 miles (480km). It requires dedicated equipment to either print the messages or display them on-screen. The main advantage of this source of data is that there is no need to listen at a particular time, as messages are automatically recorded. The main disadvantage is the cost of the dedicated equipment.

Weatherfax

Weatherfax is similar to Navtex, except the data is presented in chart rather than text form. Dedicated equipment is required for its reception. A viable alternative to this specialized equipment is to connect a personal computer to a suitable radio. With the correct software, this will enable Weatherfax data to be recorded and displayed. The same arrangement will often also record Navtex messages.

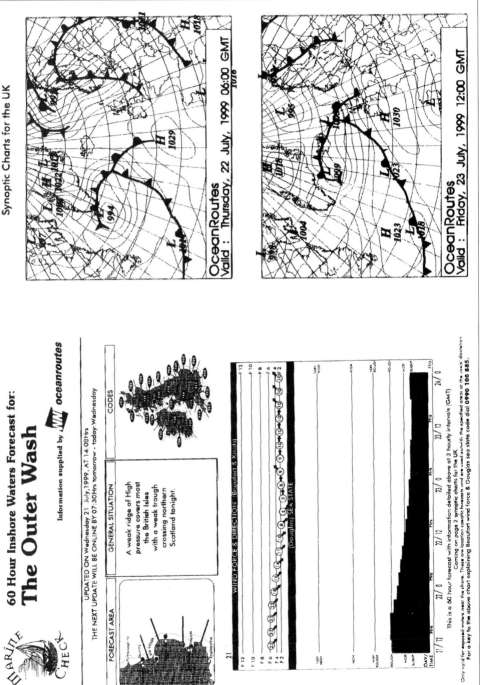

Fig. 60 Typical information available by facsimile.

Consultancy Services

Sometimes a yachtsman may want, and be prepared to pay for, a customized service. This may be from a meteorological organization or from an individual consultant meteorologist. In the United States it is quite normal for meteorologists to advertise their services alongside larger organizations; in Europe this is less common. This situation will probably change, but in the meantime private and state-owned organizations, operating on a global basis, offer individually tailored services or direct contact with a meteorologist. The main application for this type of service is for long-distance racing. Advising a yacht's crew on their optimum route for crossing an ocean with favourable winds is just a variation on advising shipping companies on safe and fuel-efficient routes for cargo vessels. This is a well-established and commercially successful business, and a yachtsman seeking competitive advantage or a good passage over shorter distances may find that the undivided attention of an individual meteorologist proves to be of good value.

Accuracy of Weather Forecasts

If a weather forecast is going to be a useful guide for the yachtsman planning a passage or race strategy, or just deciding whether or not to sail, then its reliability must be borne in mind. Unfortunately, the providers of weather services, both in the private and public sectors, are somewhat vague regarding the quality of their products. The UK Meteorological Office claims an 85 per cent level of accuracy for forecasts issued to mariners. This figure is based on a study in which meteorologists aimed to judge, with hindsight, if a predicted gale warning was appropriate or if gales had in fact occurred in the absence of a gale warning. While this information is useful to forecasters wishing to assess their own performance or the effects of changes in their procedures and techniques, it is less useful to the customer since it provides no indication of forecasting reliability in relation to lower wind speeds. It may not even give an accurate estimate of the chances of an individual yachtsman experiencing a gale if a warning is issued, or indeed of escaping gales if no warning is given. Even if a warning is judged to be reasonable, it does not mean that all yachtsmen in a given area will actually experience a gale. A study published in 1996 assessed shipping forecast accuracy from the opposite point of view by evaluating the chances of actual weather matching a forecast. It concluded that there was approximately a 64 per cent chance of wind speed and direction strength being consistent with a forecast issued 12 hours previously. It also found that extremes of wind speeds, both strong winds and calms, were less reliably forecast than winds nearer to the norm for an area. The UK Meteorological Office annual report and accounts of 1996/1997 gave a similar figure of 65.5 per cent for extreme winds in the North Sea being consistent with forecasts.

No evidence has been found to support the popular belief that forecast wind speeds tend to be exaggerated. Since most shipping forecasts give a wide range of speeds, usually about three Beaufort scales, and usually take no account of sea breezes or other important local effects, they are probably best used solely as a warning service.

Visibility, which is only presented as a warning in shipping forecasts and with very little detail, is generally forecast more accurately. Other information in the broadcast shipping forecast, such as the general synopsis and station reports, remains a very important source of background information.

Alternative forecasts are unlikely to be much better than the shipping forecast, although the more detailed inshore forecasts or local radio forecasts may have some advantages.

Making the Most of the Shipping Forecast

However a yachtsman may judge the reliability of the broadcast shipping forecast, it still remains the traditional source of weather information at sea in UK waters. Despite the fact that information is now available from so many other sources, listening to the shipping forecast, which is something of a ritual for many yachtsmen, is still worthwhile. The shipping forecast crams a huge amount of information into a very limited transmission time, but to use it properly does require a little preparation and background knowledge.

For all broadcast forecasts, noting down the information is crucial since memory and concentration are unreliable and having someone on board who is able to give their undivided attention to the radio is often something of a luxury. Most yachtsmen will be familiar with the situation in which they are standing by to catch the shipping forecast when some distraction, be it a wind shift or another vessel approaching, draws their attention away at the crucial moment and, before they know

it, the relevant information is long gone. Clearly, the average cruising yachtsman is going to need unusual discipline or mental dexterity to capture accurately a broadcast weather forecast.

To add to the difficulties, the forecast is read at a pace that is faster than normal dictation and even someone skilled in the disappearing art of shorthand would experience problems. Proformas and pre-pared blank charts obviously help, and will be discussed in greater depth later, but even with these available it is hard to cope with the unexpected. In their efforts to make the most of the limited time available forecasters will often divide up sea areas or add some detail of timing of changes in the weather that can trip up any procedure. A tape recorder is probably essential if the full forecast is to be analysed reliably (*see* Fig. 61). Some models have a timer to allow recording at pre-set times. This feature can avoid the need for waking up unpleasantly early or delaying a run ashore. It is also useful at sea as a back-up to pen and paper since forecasts can easily clash with race starts or manoeuvres when all of a yacht's crew is occupied.

Even with the forecast recorded, there is still advantage to be gained in putting it down on paper. The easiest way of doing this is to use the pre-prepared charts already mentioned. For example, the Royal Yachting Association and the Royal Meteorological Society have produced a blank chart called the 'Metmap', which allows for a great deal of added extra information. It includes average sea surface temperatures for February and September and geostrophic wind scales. The sea temperatures are intended to give the yachtsman a guide to likely sea fog formation, assuming some knowledge of air

Fig. 61 A combined radio and tape recorder with built-in timer; one of the most useful pieces of meteorological equipment on board a yacht!

temperatures and humidity. The geostrophic wind scales are based on the relationship between wind speed and pressure gradient (equivalent to the spacing between isobars on a weather chart), assuming there are no complications such as surface friction, curved isobars or accelerating airflow. This additional information is probably much too sophisticated for most yachtsmen and even some meteorologists may be sceptical of the assumptions involved. For instance, there are often quite extensive areas of unusually warm or cool water around our coasts and there is a large variation in surface wind speeds resulting from the same geostrophic wind. The geostrophic scales shown may give a very rough idea of geostrophic wind speed and speed of movement of fronts, but these figures will not be as accurate as the values derived and forecast by whoever composed the broadcast. Apart from their experience and training, professional forecasters will have available patterns of isobars based on computer analysis of large numbers of observations as well as data on the temperature structure of the atmosphere. This will allow them to anticipate the actual surface wind more accurately. Similarly, the forecaster will be able to use real sea surface temperatures in assessing the risk of fog rather than the climatic mean values written on the chart. In practice, all the yachtsman needs is a clear and simple aid to noting and analysing a weather broadcast. Other, simpler designs of prepared blank charts are available either as packs from chandlers or in popular almanacs. Having said this, the Metmap, for all its sophistication, is very convenient to use since its layout includes spaces to write out both forecast data and station reports.

Most people have their own methods or abbreviations for use with these charts. For example, a vertical line may be used to join sea areas that are linked in the forecast. A similar line can be used to mark areas with gale warnings. Likewise, an arrow can be used to denote 'becoming' and a vertical line after a record to denote 'at first'. Other abbreviations commonly used in writing down the forecast are generally self-evident – 'occ r' for 'occasional rain', and so on. There is a standardized system known as 'Beaufort Letters' that provides a means of recording weather concisely and unambiguously. Table 7 shows the Beaufort Letters most likely to be needed for noting weather conditions in shipping forecast station reports. Descriptions such as 'fair' or 'mainly fair' are probably best ignored as being of no significance other than to indicate the lack of anything more noteworthy.

The various terms used for pressure tendency (pressure tendency is the meteorological term used for the change in pressure over a previous period, usually 3

Table 7

Beaufort letters recommended as abbreviations for weather reports

Beaufort Letter	Meaning
d	Drizzle
r	Rain
s	Snow
h	Hail
tl	Thunderstorm
p	Shower
jp	Adjacent precipitation or precipitation within sight
f	Fog
jf	Adjacent fog or fog within sight
z	Haze or smoke
l	Lightning
q	Squall

Notes:
1. Intermittent precipitation is indicated by an 'i' prefix (also used for 'occasional', 'recent' or precipitation 'at times').
2. Intensity is indicated by a 'o' suffix for slight precipitation and capitals are used for heavy precipitation.
3. Letters may be combined. For example: iRS = intermittent heavy rain and snow; ir_o = intermittent slight rain.

Table 8

Terms used to describe pressure tendency and a shorthand for noting them down

Term	Meaning	Recommended Shorthand
Steady	Change less than 0.1hPa in the last three hours	
Rising more slowly	Reduction in rate of rise or change from rising to steady	
Now rising	Change from steady or falling to rising in the last three hours	
Rising slowly	Rising between 0.1hPa and 1.5hPa in the last three hours	
Rising	Rising between 1.6hPa and 3.5hPa in the last three hours	
Rising quickly	Rising between 3.6hPa and 6.0hPa in the last three hours	
Rising very rapidly	Rising more than 6.0hPa in the last three hours	
Falling more slowly	Reduction in rate of fall or change from falling to steady	
Now falling	Change from steady or rising to falling in the last three hours	
Falling slowly	Falling between 0.1hPa and 1.5hPa in the last three hours	
Falling	Falling between 1.6hPa and 3.5hPa in the last three hours	
Falling quickly	Falling between 3.6hPa and 6.0hPa in the last three hours	
Falling rapidly	Falling more than 6.0hPa in the last three hours	

hours), can be recorded in a simple short-hand. 'Falling', for example, is a simple diagonal line, but 'falling slowly' is a shallow diagonal line that does not reach the corners of the box in the proforma. The exact meaning of these terms, and a shorthand for noting them, is shown in Table 8.

Most of the terms used in shipping forecasts have well-defined meanings and are described in any good almanac. These also have the latest times of transmission of shipping forecasts (and other weather information available at sea by radio). The plotting of wind directions needs some care. A compass rose is printed on the Metmap chart, but the chart projection is such that the direction of north varies in relation to it over the area covered. The yachtsman should therefore judge directions by eye using the nearest line of longitude (such as those used to define sea areas), and should not transfer directions from the printed compass rose with parallel rules or any similar plotting device. Note also that wind direction in the UK shipping forecast is given to an accuracy of plus or minus 45 degrees and station reports are given using a thirty-two point compass rose. Wind speed is easily plotted as a line from the station with a number of 'flights' to indicate the Beaufort force. The importance of this, together with some of the strengths and weaknesses of the shipping forecast, can be illustrated by taking a couple of real examples and studying them in depth. These examples were not chosen in order to illustrate any particular 'textbook' weather pattern but were selected more or less at random. They do, however, represent two completely different situations, one of generally light winds and high pressure, issued at 1700 British Summer Time (BST) on 20 September 1997, and one of generally

strong winds and low pressure, issued at 1305 BST on 7 October 1997.

The shipping forecast issued at 1700 BST on 20 September 1997 is shown as a transcript in Fig. 62 and recorded as a Metmap in Fig. 63. This illustrates several important points, the first of which is the need for a very good recording method. The unexpected divisions of sea areas Bailey, Sole and Finisterre would trip up all but the quickest recording technique.

The station reports are for 1600 BST, whereas the general synopsis was for 1300 BST. This difference is not unusual and may be up to 6 hours for some broadcasts. This is because the Meteorological Office transmits the most recent station reports available, but means that they cannot be compared directly with the general synopsis. In a rapidly changing situation, the differences between them can be enormous. There is an added complication in that, because of technical problems, a particular station report may even be for a different time to the others (this will always be made clear during the broadcast).

Figure 64 shows the meteorological chart for 1300 BST or 1200 Greenwich Mean Time (GMT)/UTC (UTC or 'Universal Time' is effectively the modern equivalent of GMT and is widely used by meteorologists). These charts are often known as 'synoptic charts'. A synoptic chart based on real data rather than a forecast may be referred to as an 'actual'. In this case, the 'actual' appears extremely complex compared to the general synopsis. None of the fronts or other features appear in the general synopsis. This is usual and is due mainly to the very short time available to the forecaster to summarize the situation. Note, however, that there is no guarantee that the 'actual' shown is correct beyond doubt. Different

A Transcript of the Shipping Forecast Issued at 1700 BST on the 20 September 1997

'... the shipping forecast issued by the Meteorological Office at 1700 on Saturday the 20th September 1997.

The general synopsis at 1300:
High, Dogger, 1033, expected German Bight 1030 by 1300 tomorrow.
Low West Sole, 1008, expected just west of Shannon, 1013 by same time.

The area forecasts for the next 24 hours:

Viking, North Utsire: West or north-west, 4 or 5, Occasional rain, Moderate or Good.
South Utsire: North-westerly 4 or 5, Fair, Good.
Forties: Westerly 3 or 4, Fair, Good.
Cromarty, Forth: Variable, mainly south or south-west 3, Fair, Good.
Tyne: South-easterly 3, Fair, Good.
Dogger: Variable 2 or 3 becoming west or south-west 3, Fair, Good.
Fisher: North-westerly 4 or 5, Mainly fair, Good.
German Bight: North or north-west 3 or 4 becoming variable 3, Fair, Good.
Humber: Easterly 3 or 4, Fair, Good.
Thames, Dover: East or north-east 4 or 5, occasionally 6 in Dover at first, Fair, Good.
Wight, Portland: Easterly 4 or 5, occasionally 6 at first, Occasional rain, Moderate, occasionally poor.
Plymouth: Easterly 4 or 5, occasionally 6 becoming variable 3 or 4, Thundery rain at times, Moderate with fog patches.
Biscay: Variable, mainly north-westerly 3 or 4, Thundery showers.
South East Finisterre: North or north-west 3 or 4, occasionally 5 near Cape Finisterre, Showers, Moderate or good.
Northwest Finisterre, West Sole: South-westerly 4 or 5 occasionally 6 at first, Showers, Good.
East Sole: Southerly 3 or 4, Showers, Moderate or good.
Lundy, Fastnet: South-easterly 4 or 5, Showers, Moderate, occasionally poor.
Irish Sea: East or south-east 4 or 5, occasionally 6 at first, Occasional rain in south, Moderate or good.
Shannon: East or south-east 4 or 5, occasionally 6, Mainly fair, Moderate or good.
Rockall, Malin: East or south-east 3 or 4, occasionally 5 in south, Mainly fair, Moderate or good.
Hebrides, South Bailey: Variable, mainly south-easterly 3 or 4, Fair, Good.
North Bailey: South-westerly 4 or 5, Fair, Good.
Fair Isle: Westerly 4 or 5, Mainly fair, Good.
Faeroes, South East Iceland: West or south-west 4 or 5, occasionally 6 at first, Mainly fair, Moderate or good.

Now the weather reports from coastal stations at 1600 BST:

Tiree: South-east 3, 16 miles, 1028, Falling slowly.
Stornoway: South-south-east 2, More than 38 miles, 1028, Falling slowly.
Lerwick: West by north 4, 22 miles, 1029, Falling slowly.
Bridlington: South-east by east 4, 16 miles, 1031, Falling slowly.
Sandettie Light Vessel automatic: North-east by north 5, 11 miles, 1027, Falling.
Greenwich Light Vessel automatic: North-east 5, 5 miles, 1027, Falling slowly.
Jersey: East-north-east 4, 7 miles, 1023, Now rising.
Channel Light Vessel automatic: East by north 6, 2 miles, 1024, Steady.
Scilly automatic: East by south 4, 2 miles, 1022, Rising slowly.
Valentia: East-south-east 3, intermittent slight drizzle, 5 miles, 1020, Falling slowly.
Ronaldsway: East by south 4, 6 miles, 1028, Falling slowly.
Malin Head: East-south-east 3, 16 miles, 1026, Falling slowly.'

Fig. 62 A transcript of the shipping forecast issued at 1700 BST on 20 September 1997.

RYA / R Met Soc Metmap

GENERAL SYNOPSIS 20.9.97 at 1300 GMT (BST)

H, Dogger, 1033, expected German Bight 1030 by 1300 tomorrow, L, West Sole, 1008 expected just west of Shannon, 1013 by same time.

Gales	SEA AREA FORECAST	Wind	Weather	Visibility
|	Viking	W or NW 4/5	ir	m, g
	N. Utsire			
	S. Utsire	NW ly 4/5		g
	Forties	W ly 3/4		g
|	Cromarty	Var. main S/SW 3		g
|	Forth			g
	Tyne	SE ly 3		
	Dogger	Var. 2/3 → W/SW 3		g
	Fisher	NW ly 4/5		g
	German Bight	N or NW 3/4 → Var. 3		g
	Humber	E ly 3 or 4		g
|	Thames	E or NE 4 or 5 occ 6 in		g
	Dover	Dover 1		
|	Wight	E ly 4 or 5 occ. 6 |		g
|	Portland			
	Plymouth	E ly 4 or 5 occ. 6 Var. 3 or 4		m, f p
	Biscay	Var., mainly NW ly 3 or 4		m
	~~Trafalgar~~			
	Finisterre SE ~~Finisterre~~ N or NW	N or NW 3 or 4, occ. 5 near Cape 5	p	m or g
	Sole W ~~E Sole~~	SW ly 4 or 5 occ 6 |	p	g
	Lundy	E ly 3 or 4		m or g
|	Fastnet	SE ly 4 or 5	p	m, occ. p
	Irish Sea	E or SE 4 or 5, occ. 6 |	ir in S	m or g
	Shannon	E or SE 4 or 5, occ. 6		m or g
|	Rockall	E or SE 3 or 4, occ 5 in S		
	Malin			
	Hebrides (~~Bailey~~ S)	Var. mainly SE ly 3 or 4		g
	Bailey N	SW ly 4 or 5		g
	Fair Isle	W ly 4 or 5		g
|	Faeroes	W or SW 4 or 5, occ 6 |		m or g
	SE Iceland			

COASTAL REPORTS (Shipping Bulletin) at 1600 (BST) ~~GMT~~	Direction	Force	Weather	Visibility	Pressure	Trend
Tiree	SE	3		16	1028	\
Stornaway	SSE	2		>38	1028	\
~~Sumburgh~~ Lerwick	W by N	4		22	1029	\
Fife Ness						
Bridlington	SE by E	4		16	1031	\
~~Dover~~ Sandettie	NE by N	5		11	1027	\
Greenwich LV Auto	NE	5		5	1027	\
Jersey	ENE	7		7	1023	—
Channel LV Auto	E by N	6		11	1024	—
Scilly Auto	E by S	4		2	1022	—
Valentia	ESE	3		5	1020	\
Ronaldsway	E by S	4		6	1028	/
Malin Head	ESE	3		16	1026	\

11/95

COASTAL REPORTS (Inshore Waters) at .... BST/GMT					
Boulmer					
Bridlington					
Walton on the Naze					
St Catherine's Point					
Scilly Auto					
Mumbles					
Valley					
Liverpool Crosby					
Ronaldsway					
Killough					
Larne					
Machrihanish					
Greenock					
Benbecula Auto					
Stornoway					
Lerwick					
Wick Auto					
Aberdeen					
Leuchars					

Fig. 63 A Metmap record of the shipping forecast issued at 1700 BST on 20 September 1997.

forecasters, agencies or companies often have different interpretations of the meteorological situation. If this seems strange then a look over the weather maps in a collection of a single day's quality newspapers, especially if other European titles are included, will prove the point, as even major features can differ in scale and location according to the origin of the report. The plot of station reports for 1600 BST in Fig. 65 also fails to give many clues to these extra features. The drizzle reported from Valentia might suggest the presence of a front or trough. The pressure variations from the station reports are somewhat contradictory and give no clear signs

of fronts, perhaps because the low and the associated fronts are relatively weak features. The central pressure, 1,008hPa, which is not very low and which is forecast to rise, suggests a decaying system. The retrograde (east to west) motion of the low is also characteristic of an old feature.

The forecast gives an overall picture of high pressure dominating most of the country with a decaying frontal depression in the west, but begs the question 'How accurate were the predictions for the next 24 hours?' The winds from station reports for 0400 BST on 21 September, about 12 hours after the forecast was issued, and the forecast winds themselves, are shown in Fig. 66. In

Fig. 64 Synoptic chart for 1200 UTC (1300 BST) on 20 September 1997.

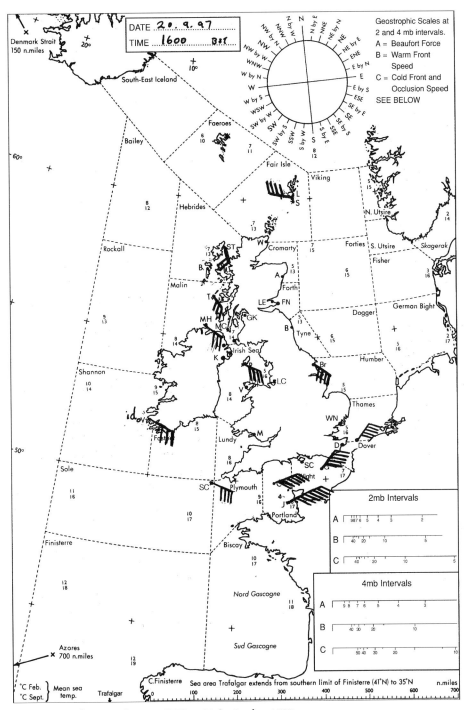

Fig. 65 Coastal reports for 1600 BST on 20 September 1997.

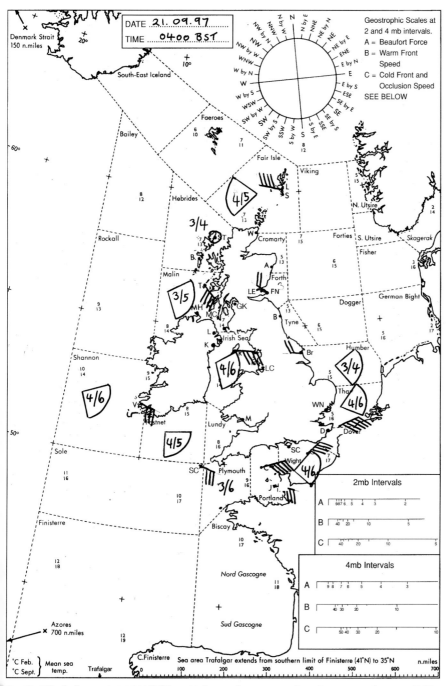

Fig. 66 Winds forecast at 1700 BST on 20 September 1997 and station reports for 0400 BST on 21 September 1997.

general, the agreement between the actual reports and the forecast is very good, with the only significant anomaly being at Bridlington. The forecast for sea area Humber was easterly three or four, whereas Bridlington is in fact reporting an offshore force two. Possibly this is due to a land breeze. Visibilities reported were all 'good', except for Valentia where the visibility of 4nm would be classed as 'moderate'. These were all in agreement with the forecast, although several sea areas had poorer visibilities mentioned as possibilities.

The shipping forecast issued at 1305 BST on 7 October 1997 is shown as a transcript in Fig. 67 and recorded as a Metmap in Fig. 68. It also has some traps for the yachtsman trying to copy down the forecast as transmitted. The visibility for German Bight and Humber, for example, ends, 'but poor at first in German Bight', which could result in confusing notes, as well as putting some burden on the space available on the Metmap.

The station reports are, in this case, 5 hours later than the synopsis, being for 1200 BST and 0700 BST respectively. Figure 69 shows the synoptic chart for 0700 BST. The broadcast synopsis has the position of the low, west of North Rockall but none of the troughs or fronts. The plotted station reports, Fig. 70, give few clues to anything other than low pressure north of Scotland. They do, however, show the strong westerly flow over southern Britain. The calm at Ronaldsway is a curiosity, all the more so because this station is manned rather than automatic and is at a busy airport and so it is most unlikely to be due to undetected instrument error. The light winds at Lerwick, Fife Ness and Bridlington presumably represent the shallow pressure gradient ahead of the low pressure area.

The forecast gave gale warnings for sea areas along the Eastern Channel and these seem to have been justified. Figure 71 shows station reports for 2300 BST and forecast wind speeds. Even if no station reported force eight at the reporting times, Sandettie, Greenwich Light Vessel and Channel Light Vessel all reported winds between force five and seven at both 1200 BST and 2300 BST. The winds at Valentia (light) and Scilly (from south by east) are curious, but may be related to air currents associated with the showery conditions. At 2300 BST every station was reporting visibility classed as 'good', again consistent with the forecast. Overall, the forecast gave yachtsmen a realistic idea of what to expect.

The two shipping forecasts described illustrate some important points. They would both be extremely difficult to record in detail without the use of a tape recorder, but in each case they gave an overview of the weather situation that was a lot easier to understand from looking at the plotted charts. Clearly, a lot can be gleaned from the information in the broadcast shipping forecast, but there is a case for simplifying it and it seems unlikely that anyone other than a real weather enthusiast would make full use of the facilities of the Metmap or gain a more accurate forecast as a result.

Adding Detail to Broadcast Weather Forecasts

At first glance, the idea of a yachtsman preparing a forecast to compete with the product of a professional organization is very unlikely. In fact, there are several circumstances in which a well-informed yachtsman can improve on the commercial product and create superior local forecasts

A Transcript of the Shipping Forecast Issued at Midday on the 7th October 1997

'... the shipping forecast issued by the Meteorological Office at 1305 on Tuesday the 7th October 1997. There are warnings of gales in Thames, Dover, Wight, Biscay, Finisterre and Rockall.

The general synopsis at 0700:

Low 300 miles west of North Rockall, 976, expected South Bailey 980 by 0700 tomorrow.
New low expected just north of Faeroes, 981, by same time.
Another new low expected just west of Sole, 991, also by that time.

The area forecasts for the next 24 hours:

Viking, North Utsire, South Utsire: South-easterly, 7 veering south-westerly 4 or 5, Rain then showers, Moderate or poor becoming good.
Forties: South-easterly soon veering south-westerly 3 or 4 increasing 5, Moderate or poor becoming good.
Cromarty, Forth, Tyne, Dogger: South-westerly 3 increasing 5 occasionally 6, Showers, Good.
Fisher: South-easterly veering south-westerly 4 or 5 occasionally 6, Rain then showers, Moderate or poor becoming good.
German Bight, Humber: South-westerly 5 to 7, Squally showers, Moderate or good but poor at first in German Bight.
Thames, Dover, Wight: South-westerly 6 to gale 8, decreasing 5 for a time, Squally showers then rain, Good becoming moderate or poor.
Portland, Plymouth: South-westerly 6 or 7, decreasing 4 for a time and perhaps gale 8 later, Squally showers, Good becoming moderate or poor.
Biscay: South-westerly 4 or 5 increasing 7 or gale 8 in north-west, Showers then rain in north, Good becoming moderate or poor in north.
Finisterre: South-westerly 5 or 6, increasing 7 or gale 8, Rain at times, Moderate or good becoming poor in north-west.
Sole: South-westerly 6 or 7 decreasing 4 for a time, perhaps gale 8 later, Squally showers then rain, Good becoming moderate or poor.
Lundy, Fastnet: South-westerly 5 to 7 decreasing 4, Showers, Good.
Irish Sea: South-westerly 4 occasionally 5, Showers, Good.
Shannon, Rockall: South-westerly 5 to 7, increasing gale 8 for a time in South Rockall, Showers, Good.
Malin: South-westerly 4 or 5, increasing 6, Showers, Good.
Hebrides: Southerly 4 increasing 5 or 6, Showers, Good.
Bailey: South-easterly backing north-easterly 4 or 5 becoming cyclonic in south, Showers, Good.
Fair Isle, Faeroes: Variable, mainly southerly 4, Rain or showers, Moderate with fog patches.
South East Iceland: North-easterly 4, Rain or showers, Moderate or good.

Now the weather reports from coastal stations at 1200 BST:

Tiree: South by east 4, Precipitation within sight, 16 miles, 987, Falling more slowly.
Stornoway: South by west 4, Precipitation within sight, 13 miles, 987, Falling slowly.
Lerwick: South-east 2, mist, 1200 metres, 989, Falling slowly.
Fifeness: South-west 2, 11 miles, 990, Falling slowly.
Bridlington: South by west 3, 7 miles, 990, Falling slowly.
Sandettie Light Vessel automatic: South-west by west 7, 1000 metres, 997, Rising slowly.
Greenwich Light Vessel automatic: South-west 7, Greater than 27 miles, 998, Rising slowly.
Jersey: West by south 6, showers, 3 miles, 1001, Rising.
Channel Light Vessel automatic: South-west by west 5, greater than 27 miles, 998, Rising.
Scilly automatic: South-west 5, 13 miles, 997, Rising.
Valentia: South-west by west 4, precipitation within sight, 11 miles, 991, Rising slowly.
Ronaldsway: Calm, 22 miles, 991, Rising slowly.
Malin Head: South 4, 38 miles, 987, Falling slowly.'

Fig. 67 A transcript of the shipping forecast issued at 1305 on 7 October 1997.

RYA / R Met Soc Metmap

GENERAL SYNOPSIS	7.10.97	at 0.700 GMT/BST

L. 300 M west of N. Rockall, 976 → S. Bailey 980 by 0700. New L
just N of Faroes, 981 by same time, New L just W of Sole, 991 by same time

Gales	SEA AREA FORECAST	Wind	Weather	Visibility
	Viking	SEly 7 → SWly 4/5	r → p	m/p → g
	N. Utsire			
	S. Utsire			
	Forties	SEly soon SWly 3/4 → 5	r → p	m/p → g
	Cromarty			
	Forth	SWly 3 → 5 occ. 6	p	g
	Tyne			
	Dogger			
	Fisher	SEly → SWly 4/5 occ 6	r → p	m/p → g
	German Bight	SWly 5/7	q p	m/g (lp in G. Bight)
	Humber			
	Thames	SW 6/8 dec 5 for a time	q p → r	g → m/p
	Dover			
	Wight			
	Portland	SWly 6/7 dec 4 for a time, perhaps 8/1	q p	g → m/p
	Plymouth			
	Biscay	SW 4/5 → 7/8 in NW	p (→ r in N)	g / m
	Trafalgar			
	Finisterre	SW 5/6 → 7/8	i r	m/g
	Sole	SWly 6/7 → 4 for a time, perhaps 8/	q p → r	g → m/p
	Lundy	SWly 5/7 → 4	p	g
	Fastnet			
	Irish Sea	SWly 4 occ. 5	p	g
	Shannon	SW 5/7 (→ 8 for a time in S. Rockall)	p	g
	Rockall			
	Malin	SWly 4/5 → 6	p	g
	Hebrides	Sly 4 → 5/6	p	g
	Bailey	SEly → NEly 4/5 → cyclonic in S	p	g
	Fair Isle	Var., mainly Sly 4	r/p	m, f p
	Faeroes			
	SE Iceland	NEly 4	r/p	m/g

COASTAL REPORTS (Shipping Bulletin) at 1200 BST/GMT	Wind		Weather	Visibility	Pressure	Trend		COASTAL REPORTS (Inshore Waters) at .... BST/GMT
	Direction	Force						Boulmer
								Bridlington
								Walton on the Naze
Tiree	S by E	4	j p	16	987			St Catherine's Point
Stornaway	S by W	4	j p	13	987			Scilly Auto
Symburgh Lerwick	SE	2		1200	989			Mumbles
Fife Ness	SW	2		11	990			Valley
Bridlington	SW by W	3		.7	990			Liverpool Crosby
Dover Sandethie	SW by W	7		1000	997			Ronaldsway
Greenwich LV Auto	SW	7		>27	998			Killough
Jersey	W by S	6	p	3	1001			Larne
Channel LV Auto	SW by W	5		>27	998			Machrihanish
Scilly Auto	SW	5		13	997			Greenock
Valentia	SW by W	4	j p	11	991			Benbecula Auto
Ronaldsway	calm			22	991			Stornoway
Malin Head	S	4		38	987			Lerwick
								Wick Auto
								Aberdeen
								Leuchars

11/95

Fig. 68 A Metmap record of the shipping forecast issued at 1305 on 7 October 1997.

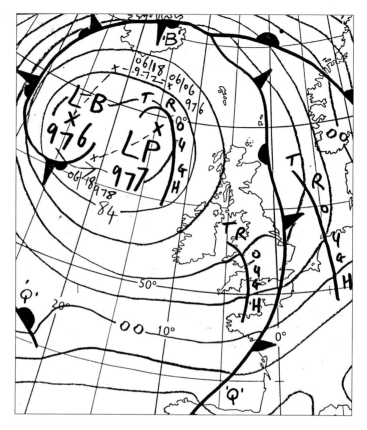

Fig. 69 Synoptic chart for 0600 UTC (0700 BST) on 7 October 1997.

for himself. One obvious example is regarding sea breezes, which rarely feature in large-scale forecasts so the yachtsman has no choice but to decide for himself if they are going to influence his sailing area. The shipping forecast will give forecast winds based on the large-scale situation. Since sea breezes require light offshore winds or calm conditions, the prediction of these provides useful clues. A land forecast mentioning warm inland temperatures or, better still, scattered showers, is indicative of rising air over land and this will encourage a sea breeze. When a light offshore wind is forecast together with warm afternoon temperatures inland the yachtsman should not be surprised by the occurrence of sea breezes, even when they have not actually been forecast.

Sea breezes are just one example of a local effect which is not covered by the usual forecasts. Meteorologists call phenomena on the scale of sea breezes mesoscale effects and they can only be studied by specialist computer models and intensive campaigns of data collection. Convergence and divergence of the wind at coastlines are also mesoscale effects, but they can at least be anticipated by the yachtsman. If the wind is approaching a steep coastline it will tend to speed up along the coast. Convergence can also be predicted if land breezes are likely to interact with a wind along the coast.

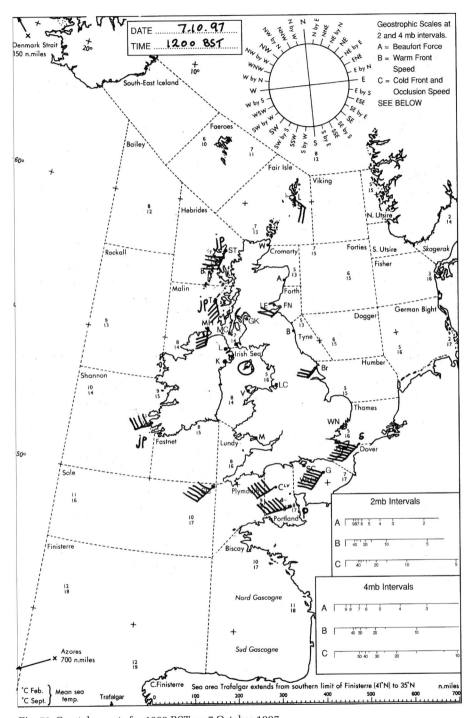

Fig. 70 Coastal reports for 1200 BST on 7 October 1997.

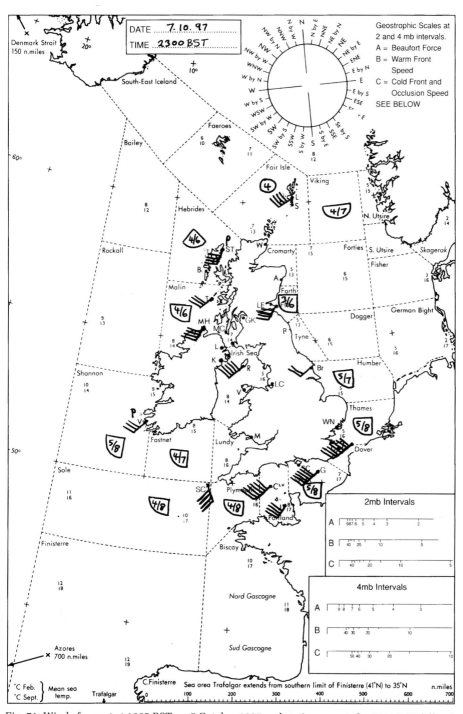

Fig. 71 Winds forecast at 1305 BST on 7 October 1997 and station reports for 2300 BST following.

Winds in the Mediterranean Sea

The Mediterranean Sea is subject to a number of local and seasonal winds. These illustrate the usefulness of local knowledge in interpreting forecasts. Often the same basic wind will have different names in different countries or regions. For example, the Scirocco, a warm, southerly wind occurring during the summer months and which brings continental, tropical air from North Africa, is called Lebeche in southern Spain, Ghibli in Libya and Khamsin in Egypt. The Khamsin wind of the eastern Mediterranean is similar in type to the Scirocco, but is more easterly with its source region in the Negev desert or even further east.

The Etesian (Greek) and Meltemi (Turkish) are local names for the northerly winds which dominate during the summer in the Aegean. These can reach as much as force six or even seven for a few days, but are usually rather less. They are driven, as are many of the predominately northerly winds of the Mediterranean summer, by a pressure gradient occurring between high pressure to the west (associated with the Azores ridge) and lower pressure to the east.

The Bora of the Adriatic is a cold, winter wind flowing down from the level of the Dinaric Alps. It is not strictly a katabatic wind, as it is sometimes described, but results from the blocking effect of the mountains holding back air at lower levels. Air from higher up then descends rapidly down the leeward side of the mountains and creates very cold winds reaching up to gale force, in a phenomenon known as a 'lee wave', which may last for several days.

The Mistral (Tramontana in Spain) is in some ways similar to the Bora, but is affected by the funnelling of air down the Rhône Valley. It can also last for several days. These winds occur most strongly and frequently during the summer months and are generally much weaker and milder in the winter.

Winds in the Strait of Gibraltar are dominated by the local terrain. The Levanter is an easterly wind which occurs at all times of the year. It is generally cool and moist and generates eddies of considerable size to the west of the rock. It may also produce a 'banner' cloud streaming downwind of the rock. Its opposite is the Vendaval, which is mainly a westerly wind occurring during the winter months.

The Apennines can also produce blocking and so create strong, cold, north-westerly winds in the Gulf of Senos and the Tyrrhenian Sea. These are known as the Tramontana (not to be confused with the Tramontana of Eastern Spain).

The map (see Fig. 72) shows some of the best-known Mediterranean winds as well as the Mediterranean Front. This feature divides the hot continental air to the south from the cooler air to the north. It is predominately a winter feature which may have a temperature discontinuity of about 15°C across it. For more detailed information and advice the reader is recommended to refer to pilot books and guides describing the area in greater depth.

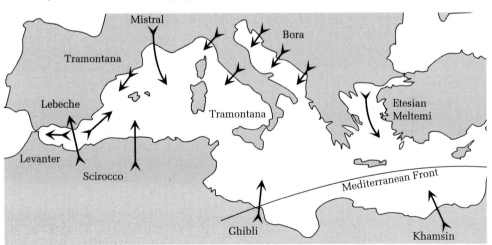

Fig. 72 Mediterranean winds.

It is also possible for the yachtsman to anticipate katabatic winds. Usually some local knowledge or a good regional guide is necessary, but the requirement of overnight cooling is a matter of judgment or careful attention to the land forecast.

It is not just local wind that is amenable to amateur forecasting. If the shipping forecast predicts coastal fog patches resulting from radiation fog inland, then the yachtsman can expect the fog to be more of a problem on windward than leeward coasts.

All of these examples relate to small-scale forecasts based on local effects. The yachtsman should never be too confident of his ability to anticipate these. Winds on a small scale, especially light winds, are highly sensitive to a variety of influences, such as local terrain and variations in surface temperatures. It is easy to be misled by deceptively simple mental pictures of wind behaviour. Deciding after the event why the wind behaved in a particular way is easy, as there is rarely any way of checking whether the explanation is correct or not.

Satellite Photographs

Yachtsmen nowadays are increasingly likely to be able to make use of satellite photographs from sources such as the Internet and television. Satellite pictures are very helpful for illustrating meteorological phenomena, but whether they are a useful aid to the yachtsman or merely an unnecessary source of confusion is open to discussion. Interpretation of satellite pictures is not as straightforward as at first it might seem. It should be noted that weather satellites do not just transmit images, they can also provide crude temperature profiles, approximate sea surface temperatures and other data from remote regions that can be of great use to professional weather forecasters. It is unlikely, though, that any of this will be of concern to the individual yachtsman with a satellite picture in his hand.

However, if the yachtsman really wants to try to make some use of these images, there are a few simple rules to observe. Firstly, check the time that the picture was taken and exactly which area is shown. The time of day is always critical to interpretation (the picture may cover an area that is in darkness). For example, at night the cold sector of a depression over land will be clear or even fog-covered, but will be full of convective cloud by the middle of the afternoon. It is also important to appreciate that the satellite looks down on the atmosphere from above, while we live and sail our boats at the base of the atmosphere. The relationship between the two is subtle. A warm front may be obvious on a satellite photograph as a brilliant streak of high-level cloud, but the surface warm front will be hundreds of miles behind it and could be difficult to spot. Another factor to be considered is whether the picture was based on recovered visible light or long-wave infra-red. The latter gives a good guide to the temperatures within the area of the picture, but the combination of the two pictures will result in very much more information than either will alone. A large white area on a visible image may be interpreted as high cloud, but if it appears dark on the infra-red image it is obvious that the cloud top is warm and thus at low altitude. It is reasonable, therefore, to assume that it may be fog or low cloud.

Probably the only yachtsmen really able to benefit from satellite imagery are those sailing in remote regions where routine forecasts are not issued. A yachtsman in such a situation might obtain a characteristic image of a tropical revolving storm that was unexpected or in a surprising location (generally it is very unlikely that a yacht would have the means to receive a satellite image but not a weather report). A sailor in a really remote region, such as the Southern Ocean, may be able to gain some insight into the location of depressions, their development or tracks, that was not available by other means. However, readers should remember that they will never be in possession of a satellite picture that is not also available to all the professional forecast providers and it is hard to see how they might pick out information that a trained and experienced professional could not. The only way they can benefit from a satellite image (other than in gaining greater understanding of meteorological phenomena), is if the professionals are not providing them with a service for their region.

Weather Folklore

A huge amount of weather folklore has evolved over the generations, some of which can be useful in making predictions about weather conditions that are correct more often than pure chance would allow. However, any meteorologist with sufficient imagination can devise explanations as to why a particular piece of folklore should be taken seriously. Ideally, folklore should be evaluated by some impartial statistical technique in the same way as conventional forecasting techniques are evaluated. This is not always easy since the actual meaning of these sayings can be extremely vague. For example, there are several rhymes suggesting that mackerel skies imply stormy weather:

Mackerel sky and mares' tails,
Make lofty ships carry low sails.

There is no universal agreement as to exactly what a mackerel sky is and various authors have taken the phrase to mean either high stratocumulus, particular types of altocumulus, or cirrocumulus clouds. Although these are different types of clouds they all imply some sort of development or instability, so this folklore is generally taken as being worthwhile. Mares' tails are probably high cirrus clouds which are not necessarily significant, unless they develop and thicken rapidly, in which case they may signify an approaching frontal depression.

Probably the most frequently quoted piece of weather lore is the saying:

Red sky at night, shepherd's delight,
Red sky in the morning, shepherd's
  warning.

Measuring sky colour is not an easy matter for anyone and what causes delight to shepherds is, in general, beyond the scope of this book. However, this saying, which goes back at least to the Gospel of St Matthew, has been evaluated scientifically. From 1918 to 1924 a gentleman called Spencer Russell observed and graded sunrise and sunset colours in London and noted whether the next 24 hours produced rain. He found that, as a predictor of a rain-free day, a red sunset was reliable on 69 per cent of occasions. This is statistically highly significant as rain is recorded on only about 50 per cent of days in the UK. However, it is not as reliable as professional forecasts which are claimed to be correct on about 80 per cent of occasions when predicting a rain-free 24 hours.

By comparison, folklore concerning halo phenomena as precursors of rain or storms are almost within the remit of conventional meteorology:

A ring around the sun spells rain.

Halo phenomena are the bright rings seen around the sun or a full moon at 22 degrees distance in the presence of cirrostratus cloud. Since this cloud is often associated with approaching warm fronts which are likely to bring rain and stronger winds, many professional meteorologists have endorsed haloes as precursors of rain. In 1972 a meteorologist called J.P. Brain analysed eighty days on which halo phenomena were observed. Only thirty of these were associated with warm fronts and only forty-five were followed by rain within 48 hours. Therefore, a piece of folklore which seems to have a completely solid scientific basis is in fact less reliable than the common red-sky rule. There is, however, a little more to this particular piece of folklore:

The larger the ring, the sooner we shall have rain.

In fact, neither the solar nor the lunar haloes vary in size. Either the folklore is based on erroneous observations, brighter haloes being seen as larger, or some distinction is being made between haloes and other phenomena.

Sometimes unlikely old folklore can surprise the professionals by being proved reliable. The best example of this is the ancient belief that waves are damped or subdued by rain. There is also a common belief that wind increases with tide, or that strong winds come in with the tide. There is actually some evidence that this is true, although the reasons for it are not clear. Perhaps a rising tide effectively reduces the drag imposed on the wind as sandbanks or low-lying marshes are covered with water.

Weather folklore is a fascinating subject in its own right, but the yachtsman wanting to know what the weather is going to bring is probably well advised to listen to the radio forecast first.

9

METEOROLOGICAL INSTRUMENTS ON BOARD

Wind Sensors

Wind sensors are probably the most common meteorological instruments to be found on board yachts. Usually, they are of the cup anemometer and wind vane type (*see* Fig. 73). Over the years, meteorologists have learnt a great deal about the performance of cup anemometers and it is now accepted that three cups are preferable to

four for establishing an even rate of rotation, conical cups are superior to spherical, and there is an optimum ratio between the cup diameter and the length of the arms that the cups are mounted on. Most of this knowledge has now filtered down to the manufacturers of those instruments offered to yachtsmen. Professional users of wind sensors must also be concerned with the response of the instruments to gusts, which

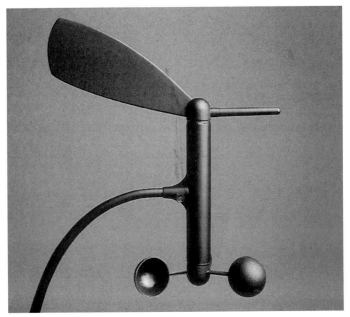

Fig. 73 A typical masthead anemometer and wind vane installation.

are measured in terms of length constants and damping ratios. However, these factors are unlikely to be of great concern to yachtsmen.

Cup anemometers have the useful characteristic of responding to wind speed irrespective of the air density. This means that a 10kt wind will produce the same response from a cup anemometer whether the air is cold and at high pressure and therefore relatively dense, or warm and at low pressure and therefore relatively less dense. Unfortunately, when installed on a yacht at sea they are prone to a host of other errors which will be discussed later. In order to be of greatest use to yachtsmen the majority of wind instruments are provided with user-friendly displays showing direction relative to the boat. Displays marked in Beaufort scales are sometimes offered, but it is unlikely that this serves any useful purpose. The Beaufort scale is defined in terms of 10-minute average wind speeds and, unless the observer is prepared to average the reading mentally or the manufacturer has supplied a means of averaging, obtaining a true wind speed on the Beaufort scale is going to be a haphazard process.

Sources of Error in Wind Sensors

For various reasons, the wind speed and direction displayed on a yacht's wind measuring system are unlikely to be close to the true value of the wind beyond the yacht. Unless the readings can be processed in some way using other data they can only show the apparent wind measured from a boat moving through the water. Another source of discrepancy is the location of the sensors themselves. The masthead is the obvious and usual location, but it is far from ideal. The sails

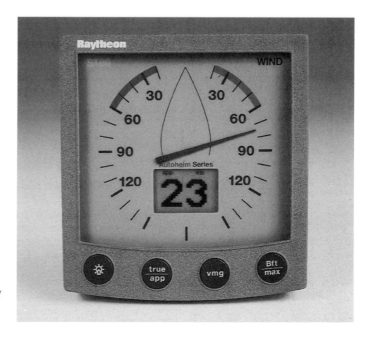

Fig. 74 A modern wind display with extended scales for close-hauled sailing.

will produce a considerable distortion of wind speed and direction at this point, typically more than 10 per cent in speed and 5 degrees in direction. Other sources of error are more subtle. For instance, as a yacht heels, the wind strikes the cups of the anemometer from below rather than directly from the side, providing that the wind flow distortion caused by the yacht allowed this to occur in the first place. The response of the anemometer to this is highly dependent on the exact shape of the sensors. The rate of rotation of the sensor may increase or decrease and it is unlikely that the manufacturers will have compensated for this, although some of the more expensive models do make a rough allowance at the higher wind speeds. Professional meteorologists are also concerned with the response of an instrument to gusts. If a sensor can speed up in response to a gust faster than it can slow down afterwards, as is usually the case, gusty winds will be exaggerated. All these finer points are not in themselves important to a yachtsman, but it is important to be aware that the wind sensors fitted to yachts have considerable limitations and should not be relied on to provide an accurate measurement of the real wind. This does not mean that the instruments have no use, only that they should be used with care and not interpreted literally.

Tactical Use of Wind Sensors

Different skippers will have different ideas about using wind sensors to advantage. Usually their tactics will require some experience of a particular vessel and its instruments in order to be effective. Indicated wind speed can provide an

objective means of deciding when to increase or to reef sail, one that is not susceptible to the effects of darkness, waves or morale on the crew's subjective impression of the wind's strength. Since wind speed indicators are unlikely to be particularly accurate, the crew will need to learn from experience which sails are appropriate for the best performance of a particular boat over a variety of indicated wind speeds. However, irrespective of their accuracy, even basic wind sensors can help a crew to detect any pattern in wind speed or direction that may prevail on a particular day.

Some of the more sophisticated wind systems available can take data from the vessel's log and calculate and display 'true wind' as opposed to apparent wind. In doing so, they compensate for the effect of the vessel's motion through the water along its set course. This will not allow for leeway or tide so the displayed wind is not strictly a true wind as a meteorologist would understand the term, but is a much better approximation than the apparent wind. This can be especially useful in showing a change in wind direction that a helmsman, concentrating on sailing as close to the wind as possible, may not notice and which could mean that a change in tack is required.

At the top end of the market, equipment is available that will take ground speed and track information from a GPS navigation system to allow calculation of wind speed and direction relative to the ground. This is often referred to as the 'ground wind'. At this level of sophistication the equipment may also permit a good deal of calibration specific to the yacht on which the equipment is installed. This usually involves the crew entering various correction factors determined by experiment for the particular boat. For example, if the true wind indicated changes consistently with the tack that the yacht is on, then there is clearly something wrong. Factors to correct this may be entered for various wind speeds. These procedures, whilst still not resulting in measurements that a meteorological purist would accept, do go a long way to allowing for some of the errors mentioned previously.

Wind systems fitted on larger racing yachts will usually calculate another parameter called velocity made good (VMG), which is the speed the yacht is making in a direction upwind. Potentially, this is a powerful aid to a yacht sailing upwind, although there are a few pitfalls in interpreting a VMG reading. Firstly, the value of VMG can always be momentarily increased by luffing into wind. The apparent improvement will be short-lived and as the yacht slows down it will be left in a worse position. Secondly, steering the yacht and trimming sails to maintain as high a VMG as possible should not distract the crew from other important factors such as tidal streams or wind shifts.

Overall, wind sensors can be a useful aid to the most efficient way to sail a yacht so long as they are not followed slavishly and there is no reliance upon their absolute accuracy.

Weight of Wind

Weight of wind is the phenomenon whereby a yacht behaves differently on different occasions despite the same wind speed being indicated by its instruments. It is as though the wind has more weight on occasions, and hence the yacht experiences greater power and heeling moment for a given wind speed. The most obvious explanation is variation in air density. Basically, higher atmospheric pressure and/or cooler air temperatures create higher density and, therefore, a greater heeling moment and drive for a given wind speed. The cup anemometers most commonly found on yachts respond to the speed of airflow irrespective of its density. This means that different heeling moments could result for the same wind speed shown by instruments. The range of density between a cold day of, for example, 5°C and a high pressure of 1,020hPa, and a warm day of 20°C and a low pressure of 980hPa is about 10 per cent. This could be large enough to be noticeable. Rain may make the wind subjectively stronger, but it has only a small effect on density compared to temperature and pressure variations.

An alternative explanation is the possibility of variations in wind speed with height over the height of a yacht's mast. This supposes that different meteorological conditions cause the wind speed to fall off towards the surface at different rates on different occasions. In principle, the wind speed is zero at the surface due to friction, but if the fall in mean speed is concentrated in a very shallow layer rather than occurring more gradually, the yacht will experience a greater force on its sails for the same masthead wind. A more gradual fall in speed will occur in lighter wind conditions over relatively cold water in a so-called stable profile. In these conditions air at the surface is cooled and so becomes denser and heavier so that a cold, stable and stagnant layer forms at the surface. Figure 75 shows how a stable profile results in lower wind speed over much of the sail for a given masthead speed. Estimating the size of this effect is difficult as there is limited real data available for analysis. Also, most sails are wider at the base than at the masthead. This means that the potential drive is greater lower down but the heeling moment is not, since reduced leverage may compensate for increasing chord. There is also a complication in that the drive and resistance of a sail is more closely related to wind speed squared than simply wind speed. This means that a 6kt wind at a particular level up the sail in unstable conditions does not produce forces twice as large on the sail as a 3kt wind in stable conditions; rather, it produces forces four times as large.

Strong winds will tend to create a more complete mixing of the wind over the height of a yacht's mast, thus preventing a stagnant layer from forming, so this explanation is probably only applicable to light winds of less than 5 to 6kt at the masthead. The resultant effect may be quite large and realistic values of wind shear could produce a halving in heeling moment for the same masthead speed as a result of very stable layers forming close to a cold sea. The effect on drive is more difficult to estimate but is likely to be larger. A trebling of

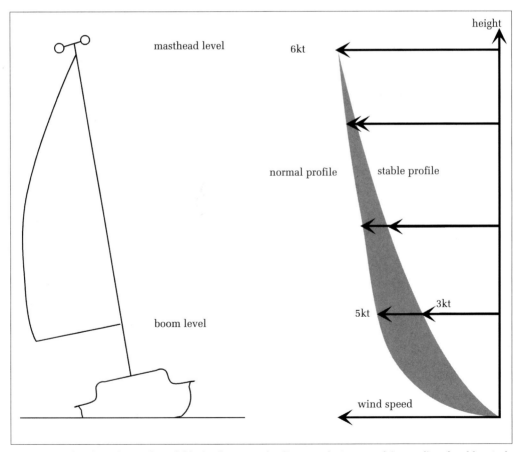

Fig. 75 Weight of wind. Wind available for driving or heeling a yacht in normal (neutral) and stable wind profiles. Shaded area represents wind unavailable from a stable profile compared to a neutral profile.

drive from the onset of increased turbulent mixing for similar masthead speeds has been quoted by experienced sailing coaches. The problem of wind shear in light airs will be exacerbated by the yacht's own movement, as the apparent wind direction at different heights will be very different, and impossibly large amounts of sail twist could be needed to get the whole sail working. On these occasions it might be worth forgetting the lower part of the sail, trimming sheets, kicking straps and so on in order to get the top of the sail, in the stronger wind, working properly.

Barometers and Barographs

Barometers are found on many yachts, though it is possible that they are as frequently used as ornaments as real guides to atmospheric conditions. Barometers and barographs will usually be marked in terms of millibars (mB), which is the traditional unit of pressure for meteorological use, although this unit is being replaced by the hectopascal (hPa). Fortunately, these units are identical, except in name, so one hectopascal equals one millibar. Station reports and weather charts issued by state meteorological offices may use either hectopascals or millibars. In practice, barometers used on yachts are unlikely to be very accurate. To give a reliable, true reading of pressure they should be calibrated at least once a year and have built-in temperature compensation. However, even if this is the case they may be prone to errors of non-linearity, meaning that even if they are accurate at one value of pressure they will be out of calibration at other values. There is also a source of error from the effect of wind blowing over the yacht. This can cause a fall in pressure

within the vessel in much the same way as the flow of air over a sail or aircraft wing causes the fall in pressure which generates drive or lift. The magnitude of this dynamic pressure, as it is called, can be over 1hPa in strong winds, but it is very dependent on the shape of the boat and its openings to the air. Suppliers of professional-grade instruments will usually offer specially designed vents to overcome this problem, but they are not really appropriate for yacht-quality instruments.

Nevertheless, a barometer can be a useful indicator of changes in pressure. A rapid rise or fall in pressure may be a very important clue as to what is happening to the weather, even if the actual value being displayed is a long way off the mark. In particular, rising pressure may indicate that a trough or front has passed and rapidly falling pressure will indicate an approaching depression, trough or front. In order to detect a change in pressure using a barometer the yacht crew must regularly record the pressure in the yacht's logbook. However, there are more modern instruments that use electronic data storage and keep an internal log of pressure changes. They are generally competitively priced, take up little room on board, and despite being less ornamental are becoming more popular with serious users (Fig. 76).

A barograph is a device which makes a continuous recording of atmospheric pressure. This is useful in that it will make changes in pressure immediately obvious, although it is still subject to the same errors as a barometer. Conventional barographs using paper, drums, pen and ink are also subject to errors due to the effects of the boat's motion disturbing the recording, although they are usually carefully designed to dampen out the motion of the boat as much as possible.

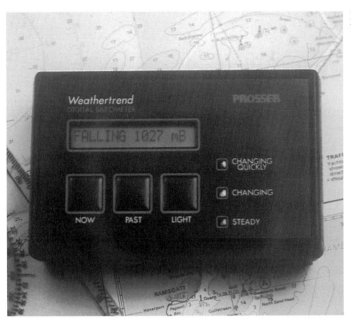

Fig. 76 A modern electronic barograph.

Other Instruments

Enthusiasts may choose to equip their vessels with any number of instruments and sensors, but other than wind and pressure sensors the only meteorological instruments likely to be of any real use are devices for measuring water temperature. Apart from trivial curiosity (Is it too cold for a swim at anchor?), water temperature can be a guide for the ocean navigator trying to find currents which may have distinctive temperatures. A naviga-tor may also be keen to avoid regions of cold water in order to reduce his chances of encountering fog or even the risk of coming across icebergs. Warmer water may sometimes be associated with stronger winds if the warmer surface initiates atmospheric convection which may prevent the surface air from becoming stagnant. This could be important in generally light winds, especially on a long voyage. For most yachtsmen, however, water temperature will be of largely academic interest.

GLOSSARY

Advection The meteorological term for the movement of air with particular characteristics. For example, if warmer air is moving into an area, then warm advection is said to be taking place.

Advection fog Fog that results from the movement (advection) of relatively warm, moist air over a cool surface (*see also* Fog).

Anemometer An instrument for measuring wind speed.

Anticyclone A region of high atmospheric pressure. The opposite term, cyclone, is usually only applied to tropical revolving storms (*see also* High).

Atmosphere The layer of gas covering the Earth.

Atmospheric stability A measure of how much the atmosphere at a given level supports or resists vertical motion. It is dependent on the rate of change of temperature with height.

Backing When a wind is described as backing, its direction is changing in an anticlockwise direction ('goes left' in dinghy sailors' jargon).

Barograph A device for measuring and displaying atmospheric pressure changes over a period of time. This may be presented either on an electronic display or as a graph drawn on paper.

Barometer A device for measuring the current atmospheric pressure.

Beaufort Scale A widely used numerical system for classifying wind strength. It is based on wind speed averaged over a 10-minute period at a height of 10m over an open surface. It was originally designed to help captains of sailing ships decide which sails to use.

Bolster eddies Eddies which form upwind of a steep obstacle or cliff (*see also* Eddies).

Buys Ballot's Law A rule of thumb which states that, 'if an observer, in the northern hemisphere, faces downwind, mean sea-level pressure will be lower in a direction to his left'. In the southern hemisphere, mean sea-level pressure will be lower to his right.

Clouds – altocumulus castellanus Convective clouds found at medium level. By indicating the presence of unstable air they often precede thundery weather.

Clouds – cirrus, cirrostratus High-level clouds composed of ice crystals.

Clouds – convective Clouds that result from instability in the atmosphere. They mark regions of air which, as a result of rising, have cooled below their dew-point temperature.

Clouds – cumulus Low-level convective clouds.

Clouds – cumulonimbus An extreme form of cumulus cloud, of great vertical extent, which usually generates thunderstorms.

Cloud street A cloud street is usually composed of cumulus clouds which have formed into distinct rows. They may mark lines of ascending air within a pattern of convection or they can even form downwind of a source, such as a power station, which is emitting large quantities of warm air.

Col A col is a region of locally uniform pressure with higher pressure on two sides and lower pressure on the other sides. It is visible as a distinct pattern of isobars on a weather chart and is usually associated with light winds. It is a term analogous to that used to describe the system of contour lines on a land map described as a col (*see also* Isobar, Trough and Ridge).

Convection In meteorological terms, convection is the pattern of rising and falling air currents that occurs in an unstable atmosphere.

Convection – closed cell Convection which organizes itself into a horizontal pattern that takes the form of solid clumps of clouds separated by narrow lines of clear air. This is particularly apparent when viewed from above.

Convection – open cell Convection which organizes itself into a horizontal pattern, taking the form of rings of clouds. This is particularly apparent when viewed from above.

Convergence Convergence occurs where more air enters a region than leaves it. At the Earth's surface an inevitable result of convergence is the ascent of air which, if the air is moist enough, often means that it is marked by cloud. The main significance to yachtsmen is that the wind speed may increase, especially if the convergence is caused by the surface wind hitting the coastline at an acute angle. A similar increase in wind speed may also result solely from the effects of local terrain in the absence of any ascent of air. Meteorologists term this phenomenon confluence (*see also* Funnelling and Divergence).

Coriolis effect The effect whereby an object, including a mass of air, moving across the rotating Earth behaves as though it is subject to a force at right angles to its direction of motion. The effect is largest at the poles, non-existent at the equator and proportional to the speed of motion. Therefore, the faster the object is moving, the greater the apparent force. In the northern hemisphere the apparent deviation is to the right of the direction of travel; in the southern hemisphere it is to the left.

Cyclone A cyclone is a tropical revolving storm occurring in the Arabian Sea, Indian Ocean or around north-west Australia with winds reaching Beaufort force twelve or above. Note that the presence of winds of force twelve, hurricane force, does not itself mean that a cyclone has occurred. The term cyclone is only used if the winds result from a tropical revolving storm (*see also* Tropical revolving storm, Hurricane and Typhoon).

Depression A region of low atmospheric pressure (*see also* Low).

Dew-point temperature The dew-point temperature of a sample of air is the temperature at which the air, when cooled, is saturated with moisture and at which condensation as fog, dew, frost or cloud particles occurs.

Divergence Divergence occurs where more air leaves a region than enters it. The main significance to yachtsmen is that the wind speed is likely to decrease. A decrease in wind speed may also result solely from the effects of local terrain in the absence of any descent of air. Meteorologists call this diffluence (*see also* Funnelling and Convergence).

Drag The retarding force felt as a result of the relative motion between an object or surface and a fluid. In meteorology it is usually applied to the effect of surface friction in retarding surface wind.

Dry Adiabatic Lapse Rate (DALR) The rate at which the temperature of air falls if it is forced to ascend through the atmosphere. Near the surface it is about 10°C per kilometre.

Eddies In meteorology eddies are regions of rotating air. They may be large, such as in hurricanes, depressions and so on, or small, such as those caused by surface friction or by obstacles to the wind. Eddies may be coherent structures or haphazard as in frictional turbulence.

Fetch The length of water which is available for wind-waves to build up. Generally speaking, if the wind has been steady for some time, the longer the fetch, the higher the waves will be up to some steady state.

Fog A suspension of water droplets or, in exceptionally cold conditions, ice crystals, that reduces visibility below 1,000m.

Fog – radiation Fog that results from the Earth's surface cooling by means of infrared radiation into space or the upper atmosphere. Air close to the surface is in turn cooled to its dew-point temperature. It is mainly a phenomenon of cool, clear nights inland, but it can on occasions spread over inshore waters (*see also* Fog and Dew-point temperature).

Fronts The boundaries between air masses with different properties.

Front – anti The term given to the band of descending air that moves seawards during the development of a sea breeze. The antifront marks the seaward extent of the sea-breeze circulation.

Front – cold A moving front with cooler air behind.

Front – occluded A moving or stationary front resulting from an overlap between a cold and a warm front. It takes the form of an elevated region of relatively warm, moist air.

Front – polar The front which divides cold polar air and warmer air from lower latitudes. It rarely exists as a complete structure and is constantly disrupted by the formation of frontal depressions.

Front – sea-breeze The boundary between a sea breeze and warmer air inland (*see also* Sea breeze).

Front – warm A moving front with warmer air behind it.

Funnelling A term used to describe the increase in wind speed which is caused by local terrain inducing convergence or confluence. It may be noticeable where wind passes through a gap in buildings or hills, or where the wind hits the coast at a narrow angle (*see also* Convergence).

Gale A period of sustained high wind. Beaufort force eight is known as a gale and means that the wind speeds, averaged over 10 minutes, are between 34 and 40kt. Force nine is known as a severe gale and means that wind speeds average between 41 and 47kt.

Gust A brief increase in wind speed above some average value.

Hectopascal A standard unit of pressure. It is numerically identical to the older millibar but is better suited to meteorological science because it is based on the universal SI system of units where the Pascal is the unit of force. A hectopascal, abbreviated as hPa, is one hundred Pascals (*see also* Millibar).

Heeling moment The heeling moment of a yacht is the effect of the wind on the sails combined with the effect of the water on the keel tending to make the boat heel over. Its size depends on the shape and set of the sails and keel and also on the values of the apparent wind speed and direction. The rate of change of wind speed with height up the mast together with the density of the air may also be significant. The latter varies with air pressure and temperature.

High A region of high atmospheric pressure (*see also* Anticyclone).

Hurricane A hurricane is a tropical revolving storm occurring in the North Atlantic with winds reaching Beaufort force twelve or greater. Note that the presence of winds of force twelve, hurricane force, does not necessarily mean that a hurricane has occurred. The term hurricane is only used if the winds result from a tropical revolving storm (*see also* Tropical revolving storm, Cyclone and Typhoon).

Isobar A line drawn on a weather map or chart which joins places of equal air pressure. For most applications the surface pressure, corrected to mean sea level, is used.

Jet stream A band of strong winds, usually in the upper atmosphere at about 9km altitude, associated with fronts marking the boundary between warm and cold air.

Lee-bow the tide A rule of thumb which is intended to provide for more efficient upwind sailing in tidal conditions. It states that if sailing upwind the tack which puts the tide coming onto the lee bow is generally preferred to one which puts the tide onto the weather bow. It is not infallible but does give some guidance on what to expect if tidal conditions are about to change.

Lee eddies Eddies which form downwind of a steep obstacle or cliff.

Loom Light which is visible when scattered from the underside of clouds even though its source may be below the horizon. It may sometimes be used to indicate the presence of navigational markers.

Low A region of low atmospheric pressure (*see also* Depression).

Mesoscale A term used to describe meteorological phenomena which occur on a scale of a few tens of nautical miles. They are smaller scale than features such as frontal depressions and include sea breezes, convergence zones and patterns associated with convection.

Millibar An outdated unit of pressure. Abbreviated as mb, it is numerically identical to the hectopascal (hPa) (*see also* Hectopascal).

Occlusion An abbreviated term for an occluded front. A moving or stationary front resulting from an overlap between a cold and a warm front. It takes the form of an elevated region of relatively warm and moist air.

Precipitation The meteorological term for any of the forms of water reaching the Earth's surface from the atmosphere. It includes rain, hail, snow, sleet and so on.

Pressure – dynamic The change in pressure at a point that results from air, or other gas or liquid, being in relative motion. It is dynamic pressure that is responsible for the action of a yacht's sail or keel. It also has some significance to pressure measurements from a barometer on a boat in a strong wind, although the effect is unlikely to be large.

Pressure gradient This is the rate of change of atmospheric pressure, usually sea-level pressure, over the surface of the Earth. It has a direction from higher to lower pressure and its magnitude represents how quickly pressure falls with distance in that direction.

Pressure – sea-level Over land, this is an imaginary pressure calculated for mean sea level which makes some assumptions about the atmosphere (it could be thought of as the pressure that might be expected in a mine whose depth matched the height of the land above sea level). For meteorological use it is calculated using the temperature of the observing station and is shown on meteorological charts. For a small boat the pressure reading of a barometer is effectively the same as sea-level pressure, although on larger vessels a correction to sea level would be applied when, for example, a barometer is mounted high up on the bridge.

Pressure – surface The pressure at the surface of the Earth due to the weight of atmosphere above.

Pressure tendency The change in pressure over a period of time (by convention 3 hours).

Ridge By analogy with height contours on land maps, a band of higher pressure visible in the pattern of isobars on a weather chart is called a ridge. They are usually associated with fair weather (*see also* Isobar, Col and Trough).

Sail chord The distance between the leading edge of a sail (luff of a jib or along the mast for a mainsail) and its trailing edge (leach) at a given level.

Sail twist The change in angle between the sail and the centre line of a yacht. For most types of rig the sail will invariably fall off downwind with height up the mast, but the amount of change can be altered by adjustment of the yacht's rigging.

Sea breeze An onshore wind generated by temperature rises inland, relative to temperature over the sea. It is part of a larger circulation of air with offshore winds aloft.

Squall A period or region (often a 'squall line') of stronger wind. Generally taken as being larger and of longer duration than an ordinary gust.

Steadman Indices The relationship between heat loss from exposed flesh and air temperature and wind speed. It allows the estimation of an equivalent or wind-chill temperature (*see also* Wind chill and Wind-chill temperature).

Surface friction The effect that a surface has on a fluid passing over it. In meteorology this refers specifically to the effect of the Earth's surface in creating drag on the surface wind.

Swell Waves that result from winds, other than those at the location and time of interest, which are blowing either at a distance or that blew in the past. They are, therefore, not related to the present winds and tend to be very regular and of longer wavelength than waves generated locally (*see also* Wind-waves).

Tropical revolving storm A region of low pressure surrounded by extreme winds that forms over warm tropical waters. It is very different to the depressions that occur in temperate latitudes as it has no fronts associated with it and is generally much smaller and more violent. If winds associated with a tropical revolving storm reach Beaufort force twelve or higher then they are referred to as a hurricane, cyclone or typhoon according to the region in which they occur (*see also under these headings*).

Trough By analogy with height contours on land maps, a band of lower pressure visible in the pattern of isobars on a weather chart is called a trough. They are usually associated with changes in wind and with increased cloud and/or precipitation. Fronts usually have an associated trough (*see also* Isobar, Col and Ridge).

Turbulence A condition where airflow breaks down into haphazard eddies. The wind at the surface is almost always turbulent.

Typhoon A tropical revolving storm in the Western North Pacific with winds reaching Beaufort force twelve or greater. Note that the presence of winds of force twelve, hurricane force, does not itself mean that a hurricane has occurred. The term typhoon is only used if the winds result from a tropical revolving storm (*see also* Tropical revolving storm, Cyclone and Hurricane).

Veering A wind veers if its direction changes clockwise ('goes right' in dinghy sailors' jargon). This is a strictly defined term in meteorology, but in common usage it may be applied to a change in direction without specifying which way the direction changes. Some care is therefore required in interpreting the word too literally.

Velocity made good The rate at which a yacht is moving upwind. This is often a critical measure of performance when a yacht is tacking upwind and some sensor systems are able to estimate it from the yacht's water speed and the apparent wind speed and direction.

Visibility Meteorologists define visibility as being the distance over which the contrast in luminance between black and white surfaces is reduced to 5 per cent. However, in popular usage visibility is generally taken as being a measure of the distance over which objects can be seen. Visibility ranges for lights shown on navigational charts are usually given assuming conditions of meteorological visibility of ten nautical miles.

Vortices A region of rotating air. It may refer, on a large scale, to a frontal depression or, on a small scale, to the disturbance downwind of a yacht's masthead. The term vortex is usually only applied to rotation which is organized in some way.

Wave length The distance between successive peaks in a system of wind-waves or swell.

Wind against tide The effect whereby waves on the sea are increased when the wind and tide are in opposing directions. There is always an effect due to the differences in relative speed between the air and water, but the effect is most dramatic when waves generated in one region travel into a region where the tide has a larger upwind component.

Wind – anabatic A wind resulting from air which is heated by contact with a warm sloped surface rising up the slope because of its reduced density (*see also* Wind – katabatic).

Wind – apparent The wind measured from a boat that is either stationary or in motion in water that may itself be moving with the current or tide. It is a combination of the true wind, the boat wind and the tide wind (*see also* Wind – boat and Wind – tide).

Wind – boat The apparent wind that is felt on a boat due to the motion of the boat through the water. Its speed is equal to the boat's speed through the water and its direction is opposite to the course through the water. In practice, it combines with the true wind and the tide wind to produce the apparent wind that acts on a boat, its sails and its crew (*see also* Wind – tide and Wind – apparent).

Wind chill This is the effect whereby moving cold air removes heat from exposed flesh more efficiently than stationary air at the same temperature (*see also* Steadman Indices).

Wind-chill temperature A temperature derived from air temperature and wind speed that gives the temperature of air at rest or at low speed that would produce the same heat loss from exposed flesh. Often derived from Steadman Indices (*see also* Steadman Indices and Wind chill).

Wind – geostrophic A theoretical wind that results from the effect of a pressure gradient together with the Coriolis effect. Strictly speaking, it only applies in the absence of friction and wind shear and to steady flow along straight isobars. Despite these conditions it is often used as a model of airflow in the free atmosphere (*see also* Coriolis effect and Pressure gradient).

Wind – katabatic A wind resulting from air cooled by contact with a cold, sloped surface sliding down the slope because of its increased density (*see also* Wind – anabatic).

Wind shear A change in wind with height. It may refer to a change in direction or speed or some combination of the two.

Wind – tide The apparent wind that is felt on a boat due to the water moving in a tidal stream or current. In practice, it is combined with the true wind and the boat wind to produce the apparent wind that acts on a boat, its sails and its crew (*see also* Wind – apparent and Wind – boat).

Wind vane An instrument for measuring wind direction, either by observation such as with a weather cock or masthead wind indicator, or by providing data to a visual display of some sort.

Wind-waves Waves resulting from the wind blowing at the present time at the location of interest, or nearly so. It is the opposite of 'swell', which are waves resulting from distant or past winds (*see also* Swell).

Wind – weight of The effect whereby differing atmospheric conditions cause a yacht to experience greater or lesser drive and heeling moment on different occasions, despite the same apparent wind being indicated on instruments or perceived by the crew (*see also* Wind – apparent and Heeling moment).

Recommended Further Reading

Chapters 1, 2 and 3

Barry, R.G. and Chorley, R.J., *Atmosphere, Weather and Climate* (Routledge, London and New York, 1992)
This has a good textbook approach which includes some mathematics and detailed references.

Empson, J.E., *Sea Breeze and Local Wind* (Cambridge University Press, 1994)
This gives a thorough treatment of seabreezes.

Lutgens, F. and Tarbuck, E., *The Atmosphere* (Prentice Hall, 1998)
This book gives a good, straightforward explanation of basic meteorology, including those aspects not directly relevant to sailing.

Chapter 4

The Open University, *Waves, Tides and Shallow Water Processes* (Pergamon Press, 1989)
The authors are not aware of many books giving clear explanations of the interaction of wind and waves. The origin of much of the knowledge in this chapter is in work carried out by, or on behalf of, the Royal Navy and recorded only in difficult-to-obtain reports. However, this volume will provide the reader with more detail on the subject.

Chapter 5

Quarrie, S., *Quarrie on Racing* (Waterline, 1991)
This is one of many books published on sail trim and the use of instruments. This example takes a realistic approach, avoiding the tendency to be dogmatic.

Chapter 8

Most good almanacs will give up-to-date information on sources of weather information.

G5, *Weather Forecasts* (RYA)
This booklet is published annually and has a particularly thorough guide to services available.

Scorer, R.S., *Cloud Investigation by Satellite* (John Wiley & Sons, 1986)
This book provides a good guide for the reader who is keen to learn more about satellite photographs.

Marriott, P.J., *Red Sky at Night, Shepherds Delight?* (Sheba Books, 1981)
A very thorough guide to weather folklore with some refreshingly objective analysis of the validity of old sayings.

INDEX